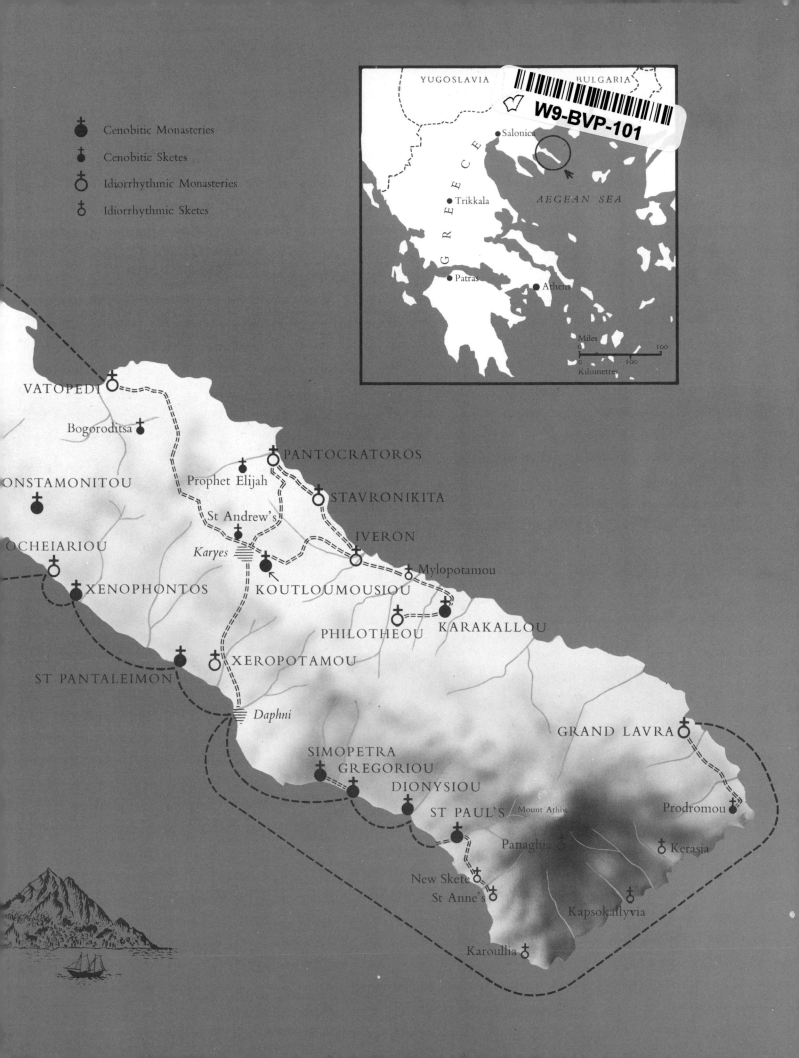

Cenobitic Monasteries

Cenobitic Sketes

Idiorrhythmic Monasteries

Idiorrhythmic Sketes

YUGOSLAVIA   BULGARIA

W9-BVP-101

Salonica

GREECE

Trikkala

AEGEAN SEA

Patras

Athens

Miles
0   100
0   100
Kilometres

VATOPEDI

Bogoroditsa

PANTOCRATOROS

ONSTAMONITOU   Prophet Elijah

STAVRONIKITA

St Andrew's

IVERON

OCHEIARIOU   Karyes

Mylopotamou

XENOPHONTOS

KOUTLOUMOUSIOU   KARAKALLOU

PHILOTHEOU

XEROPOTAMOU

ST PANTALEIMON

Daphni

GRAND LAVRA

SIMOPETRA
GREGORIOU

DIONYSIOU

Prodromou

ST PAUL'S   Mount Athos

Panaghia   Kerasia

New Skete

St Anne's   Kapsokaflyvia

Karoullia

MOUNT ATHOS

John T. Hill

MOUNT

ATHOS

BY JOHN JULIUS NORWICH
AND RERESBY SITWELL
WITH PHOTOGRAPHS BY THE
AUTHORS AND A. COSTA

HARPER & ROW, PUBLISHERS
NEW YORK

This book was designed and produced by George Rainbird Ltd., 2 Hyde Park Place, London W.2, for Harper & Row, Publishers, Incorporated. Set in 14 point "Monotype" Bembo by Richard Clay (The Chaucer Press) Ltd., Bungay, England. Plates printed by lithography by L. van Leer and Co. N.V., Amsterdam. Typographer: Ronald Clark.

Library of Congress Catalog Card Number: 66–20306

Contents

PLATES

Numerals in bold face indicate colour plates, initials denote the name of the photographer.

LETTER

Athenagoras, by the grace of God Archbishop of Constantinople, New Rome and Oecumenical Patriarch.

Ref. 447

Most Reverend supervisors of the community of the Holy Mountain, beloved children of the Lord under our Moderation, grace be to you in your Reverend office, and peace of God.

The bearers of this letter, Lord Norwich, Sir John Beckwith, Reresby Litwell [*sic*], and Constantine Achillopoulos do betake themselves to the Holy Mountain for the purpose of worship and study, with the express blessing of the Church.

Right gladly do we recommend these gentlemen to your beloved Reverences. We trust that, of your studied forethought, loving care may be everywhere afforded to the above named, and every facility for the purpose for which they are coming.

May the Grace of God, and His infinite mercy be with you in your Holy Office.

June, 3, 1964

Athenagoras
of Constantinople

"In paternal love"
"Ardent suppliant of God"

ENVELOPE

THE ROMAN PATRIARCHATE
H. Fener – Istanbul
TURKEY

Turkey

To the Right Honourable Mr Lord Norwich
c/o The British Embassy
Gennadiou and Ipsilantou
Athens
GREECE

EXPRESS

1
Letter from the Oecumenical Patriarchate with the accompanying envelope

2 (overleaf)
The monastery of Esphigmenou

'Αριθμ.Πρωτ.447.

'Οσιώτατοι 'Επιστάται καί 'Αντιπρόσωποι τῆς Κοινότητος τοῦ 'Αγίου "Ορους, τέκνα ἐν Κυρίῳ ἀγαπητά τῆς ἡμῶν Μετριότητος, χάρις εἴη τῇ ὑμῶν 'Οσιότητι καί εἰρήνη παρά Θεοῦ.

Οἱ ἐπιδόται τοῦ παρόντος κύριοι Λόρδος Νόριτζ, Σίρ Τζών Μπέκγουϊθ, Ρέρεσμπυ Λίτγουελ καί Κωνσταντῖνος 'Αχιλλόπουλος ἔρχονται, ἀδείᾳ τῆς 'Εκκλησίας, εἰς "Αγιον "Ορος πρός προσκύνησιν καί χάριν μελετῶν.

'Ασμένως τοίνυν συνιστῶντες τούτους τῇ ἀγαπητῇ ἡμῖν 'Οσιότητι ὑμῶν, προτρεπόμεθα ὅπως πρόφρονι μερίμνῃ αὐτῆς παρασχεθῇ τοῖς ἐξονομασθεῖσι πανταχοῦ φιλόφρων περιποίησις καί πᾶσα εὐκολία πρός πραγματοποίησιν τοῦ δι' ὅν ἔρχονται σκοποῦ.

'Η δέ τοῦ Θεοῦ χάρις καί τό ἄπειρον ἔλεος εἴη μετ' αὐτῆς.

αϡξδ' 'Ιουνίου γ'.

Introduction

When Reresby Sitwell, Costa and I set off for Mount Athos in the first week of June 1964 we had no intention of writing this book. There is already enough literature about the Holy Mountain to satisfy the most voracious of bibliographers, and at that time we felt neither qualified nor indeed particularly inclined to add a fresh burden to the groaning shelves. Of the three of us, only Reresby was breaking entirely new ground; Costa had had his Athonite baptism thirty years before – and actually found one old monk at the Lavra who remembered him from the former occasion – while I had made a singularly unsuccessful excursion in 1962 which, thanks to driving rain, lack of companions, inadequate preparation and a woeful ignorance of Greek, had proved less of a pilgrimage than a martyrdom. But, though we all knew something about our destination, none of us knew much; and we should, I think, have counted our journey well worth while if we had returned to the outside world with nothing more than a few good photographs, the memory of an enjoyable and instructive holiday, and a nice sun-tan.

On this level, as on others, Athos treated us kindly. A greater contrast to my earlier visit could scarcely have been imagined. The sun beat down, the sea washed our bodies and refreshed our souls. During a fortnight which was not without its quota of irritations and frustrations – and an all-male environment can have abrasive effects on the temper – we never once came to blows and I don't actually remember a cross word. We had profited by past experience and had come admirably equipped to face those rigours which are inseparable from

The ruined Tower of Milutin,
on the way to Chilandar

any Athonite journeys; and Costa's proficiency in his native tongue – unsuspected even by himself – opened many a door against which two inarticulate Englishmen would have pounded in vain. We also took prodigious quantities of photographs, an adequate but infinitesimal proportion of which will be found among the following pages. And so the days went on, and as we sank deeper and deeper under the Mountain's spell we knew that this was too rewarding a holiday to go unchronicled; it must be made to yield some tangible result, even if only a scrapbook for ourselves.

But those rewards, we also knew, went far beyond happy memories and photographs; and I for one felt that I had undergone one of the outstanding experiences of my life. For the fact is that Athos is something infinitely greater than the sum of its monasteries. It is not a community so much as a concept; and the grandeur of this concept, however misguided it may ultimately prove to be, can have a profound – at times almost a shattering – effect on those who wander within its range. They find themselves by turns entranced and revolted, bewildered and enlightened, depressed and exhilerated, terrified and consoled. Increased contact with the spiritual world brings them a new awareness of the physical. Light and sound assume a new importance for them; time and space play them tricks. As they learn more of the Mountain, so they also grow to understand more of themselves; and they emerge beset with a maelstrom of conflicting emotions and impressions that can only be resolved on paper.

So, at least, it was with us. There is, however, a third, sadder reason for this book. It is the conviction, shared by all three of us, that Athos is dying – and dying fast. In nearly every monastery the writing looms, all too plainly, on the wall. We have suggested why this should be; we have even discussed what may happen when, probably within the lifetime of most readers, the thousand-year history of the Holy Mountain comes to an end. What we have not done is to make any proposals as to how the disaster may be averted. There are none to make. The disease is incurable. There is no hope.

But meanwhile the beauty and the magic remain undiminished; and these we have tried, however quixotically, to recapture. Costa has, alas, preferred to speak only through his camera; Reresby and I have supplemented his photographs, and have split the text between us. I have started the book off with an essay on the Mountain as a whole, in which I have tried to interweave an account of its history with a general impression of how it strikes the modern traveller; Reresby has taken over with a more detailed narrative of our own particular journey. By this method we have, I hope, successfully avoided covering the same ground twice; but when, occasionally and momentarily, our paths have crossed we have made no effort to co-ordinate our views. If we contradict one another, our defence must be that on Athos where, more than anywhere else on earth, history and legend coalesce, factual truth is often unattainable and sometimes even unimportant. If we disagree, the reader must congratulate himself on having bought two views for the price of one.

John Julius Norwich

I never read of a hermit, but in imagination I kiss his feet; never of a monastery, but I could fall on my knees and kiss the pavement.

Dr Johnson

SOMETHING OF BYZANTIUM

JOHN JULIUS NORWICH

Something of Byzantium

One day in A.D. 49 the Virgin Mary, living in quiet retirement at Jerusalem, received a letter from Lazarus. It was many years, he wrote, since last they had met; he himself was now Bishop of Kitium in Cyprus, and would never return to Palestine. On the other hand, he wanted so much to see her before he died again. If he were to send a ship to fetch her, would she consent to come and visit him?

The Virgin was now in her mid-sixties. She had never – apart from a brief but essential journey to Egypt in her youth – travelled abroad. But she gladly accepted the invitation of her old friend. The ship duly arrived and bore her away to the north-east. Unfortunately the captain missed his course, and when land was eventually sighted it proved to be not the expected coast of Cyprus but the peninsula of Athos, a long and densely wooded mountain ridge that snakes down some forty miles from the Thracian Chalcidice to end in a huge pinnacle of grey marble, soaring well over six thousand feet above the sea. The ship hove to in a shallow bay, opposite the place where the monastery of Iveron now stands; it was then the site of the prosperous little town of Dion. For a long time the Virgin gazed up in silence at the peak; then she decided the future of Athos. "This mountain," she said, "is holy ground. Let it now be my portion. Here let me remain." As she stepped ashore, a great crash resounded across the peninsula; all the idols and pagan statues in Dion and the neighbouring towns fell, shattered, to the ground, proclaiming their own spuriousness at the tops of their voices and calling upon their erstwhile worshippers to hurry down to the

ILL. 29

19

water's edge, there to meet the *Panaghia*, the true Mother of God. The Virgin then baptised the entire population; and the glorious history of the Holy Mountain had begun.

Such was the story as I heard it, on my first visit to Mount Athos, from the guest-master of the monastery of Gregoriou.[1] Most of his fellow-monks, he said, believed that it could be traced back earlier still, and that Athos was that very same "exceeding high mountain" on which Christ had been tempted by the Devil;[2] on this point, however, he himself felt sceptical.

I suggested that it must have been sad for Lazarus, who had taken so much trouble, not to see the Virgin again after all.

"Yes," said the monk. "Yes, he was *very* disappointed."

*   *   *

The religious history of the Mountain in fact goes back far beyond the birth of Christ – beyond antiquity even, to the age of Chaos itself. It was the first seat of the Greek gods before they moved to Olympus, being named after Athos, Poseidon's son, who one day during a family quarrel had picked it up from its original position in central Thrace and hurled it at his father in the sea. The ancients did their best to smooth things over by vowing it to Poseidon – whose menacing trident is still plain to anyone who looks at a map of the Chalcidice – but shortly afterwards, hearing jealous rumblings from above, they hastily rededicated it to Zeus himself. Poseidon never forgave them their impertinence; ever since that time the headland of Athos has been famous for the suddenness and fury of its storms – though these, to be sure, have not always been without their uses. One particular tempest destroyed the entire fleet of King Darius in 492 B.C., dashing three hundred triremes to pieces – fifteen centuries later the monks were still fouling their nets with the débris – and thereby saved Greece for another dozen years from the Persian invaders.[3] It was to prevent a repetition

[1] The date of A.D. 49 is not generally known on Athos, where most monks, anyway, pay little heed to chronological questions. It has been ingeniously deduced by C. DE LOVERDO, an ex-monk turned journalist who accepts the legend and connects the falling of the statues with a well-documented earthquake which occurred in that year. (*J'ai été Moine au Mont-Athos*, Paris, 1956.)

[2] St Matthew, IV, 8.

[3] Herodotus, Book VI.

4
The Shrine of the Virgin
with wild madonna lilies
near Chilandar

of this catastrophe that Xerxes, Darius' son and successor, prepared for his new expedition in 480 by cutting a canal right through the neck of the peninsula; traces of it can still be made out today.

But if the soil of Athos had to yield to the inexpert shovels of Xerxes' sappers,[4] the rock itself may be congratulated on its narrow escape from the attentions of Deinocrates, court sculptor to Alexander the Great, who proposed to immortalise his master by carving the entire peak in his image, "representing him", according to the ancient Greek geographer Strabo, "as pouring a libation from a kind of ewer into a broad bowl, and to make two cities, one on the right of the mountain and the other on the left, and a river flowing from one to the other".[5] Alexander, we learn, refused his consent. It was just as well. Had this greatest of all monuments to megalomania been realised, it is unlikely that the most extraordinary religious and social experiment known to Christendom would ever have been undertaken. And yet, one can't help thinking, that man-mountain idea – it would have been rather marvellous. . . .

Although – even after a prolonged stay – Mount Athos does not in the least resemble the female breast to which Strabo extravagantly, if unfortunately, compares it, it looks, after more than two thousand years, much the same as it looked to Xerxes and Alexander. Threading his way as best he can along the tortuous and agonisingly rock-paved paths which constitute the only means of land communication between one monastery and the next – could they have been deliberately constructed as a means of mortification, or perhaps as some everpresent reminder of the roughness of the road to Paradise? – the traveller soon forgets the anguish underfoot in the beauty of what lies around him. On Athos, Nature herself seems virginal. Thanks to the stringent exclusion of females, a ban which applies not to women only but to all domestic animals, the entire peninsula has preserved a richness and luxuriance of vegetation unique in Greece and perhaps in Europe. For nearly ten centuries, perhaps longer, the fields have lain ungrazed by cattle, the trees have escaped the ravages of goats, the flowers

[4] Herodotus, Book VII. Different nationalities worked different sections. It was here that the Phoenicians showed their superiority. All other contingents dug vertically, so that the sides kept caving in. Only the Phoenicians began with a trench of double the stipulated width, sloping the walls inwards as they dug deeper.
[5] Strabo, 14, 1, 23. In some texts the sculptor is referred to as Cheirocrates, but this is almost certainly a mistake.

B

5
The great tower of the
Serbian monastery of
Chilandar

have had no children to pick them. All down its length, until that southernmost tip where the Holy Mountain itself at last breaks free of the crowding forests and rears colossal to the sky, this rocky ridge remains submerged under an endless variation of green – of oak and fir, chestnut and pine, and the little groups of hazels which long ago gave the village capital, Karyes, its name. Their colours remain vivid in the memory – as do the bursts of yellow broom above Iveron, a profusion of purple iris and orchid near Karakallou; a whole field of wild lilies   ILL. 4 round a little chapel on the way to Chilandar, where the divinely guided donkey bringing the miraculous icon of the Trikheiroussa from Serbia in 1371 fell down dead, his mission accomplished – and, embracing them all, the sparkling cobalt of the sea. Only an occasional rusty tin or mouldering cigarette carton, some sad strand of telegraph wire meandering hopelessly through the foliage, provides an unheeded reminder of the century current in the outside world – these, and the new dirt road that winds from the little port of Daphni over the ridge to Karyes, enabling a venerable bus, its windscreens impenetrably festooned with representations of the Virgin and Saints, to provide the first mechanised link between the only two villages of the Mountain – and twice a day to temper the air, summer-loud with the song of birds, insects and a thousand hurrying streams, with the gruff gurgle of imperfect internal combustion. Everywhere else, and at all other times, one might be living in the Middle Ages.

But then, of course, one is; and herein lies the secret of Athonite fascination. On the morning of May 29, 1453, just before daybreak, the Janissaries of the Ottoman Sultan Mehmet II streamed over the walls of Constantinople and brought to an end the Byzantine Empire. It had been in existence for one thousand, one hundred and twenty-three years, during most of which it had preserved, virtually alone, the heritage of European civilisation from the depre-dations of the barbarians and the long cultural night that followed. The last of its Emperors, Constantine XI, died as he had wished to die, fighting for his city; and, with his death, the light which had burned brighter, longer and more steadfast than that of any other state in European history was extinguished for ever. And yet – not quite. Mount Athos, after nearly five centuries as the spiritual centre of the Orthodox world, had submitted of her own free will to Turkish domination in 1430, when the capture of Salonica had made her position hopeless. By doing so, thanks to that Islamic tradition which rewards voluntary surrender by forbidding pillage and allowing Christians to retain their places of worship for the free exercise of their religion, she preserved not only her treasures but also her effective independence; and thus she became the only autonomous Christian community to exist under Ottoman rule. Here, and here alone, under the bored but benevolent eye of a Turkish *Agha*, the old Byzantine traditions remained alive, just as – under the somewhat testier protection of the Greek Government – they do to this day. To visit Athos, then, is to return to the Middle Ages; to live the life of a pilgrim, travelling on foot or mule-back over the rough trails between one shrine and the next, accepting whatever food and shelter may be offered by the great religious houses along the way; and to find, within those houses, communities of men whose daily life and attitude of mind are far closer to medieval Constantinople than to modern Athens.

It is a strange translation; and stranger still is the effect which it produces in the traveller's mind. Within a day or two of his arrival he, too, begins to feel its influence. It touches him at all levels. Just as his physical perception seems contained by the Mountain and the encircling sea, so his spirit is swathed in the beauty and serenity he finds around him, and his grateful mind adjusts to the deceleration of time. Miles and kilometres are forgotten; distances from one monastery to the next – and no other distances exist – are reckoned in hours or days. As this adjustment proceeds, the peninsula becomes immense; a journey between two monasteries lying almost within sight of one another can assume the proportions of a transatlantic voyage. But he does not see it in those terms. For him the outside world has slipped far, immeasurably far, away.

*   *   *

No one is quite sure when Mount Athos first became a centre for monks and hermits. The Emperor Constantine the Great is said, without a grain of evidence, to have built three churches there, all subsequently destroyed by Julian the Apostate; be that as it may, throughout the early Middle Ages the place seems to have enjoyed a certain reputation for sanctity, on which the seal was finally set in the ninth century by the arrival of its first saint, Peter the Athonite – his choice of retreat being made, it need hardly be said, on the recommendation of the Virgin, and his actual journey by her miraculous intervention. (It is a characteristic of the Mountain's history that few of its distinguished early visitors ever arrived there by normal methods; the same is true of its more important relics and icons.) Once ashore, Peter lived for thirty-five years in a cave – which may still be inspected by persons sound of wind and limb and with a head for heights – subsisting only on herbs and manna. He was followed by a certain St Euthymius of Salonica, arriving in the company of a friend with whom he at first went about on all fours eating grass. Later they moved, like Peter, to a cave, from which the friend – who had apparently managed the grass – was soon driven out by the prodigious voracity of the vermin; Euthymius, however, remained for three years, and emerged to find himself the centre of a *lavra* – one of those admiring groups of disciples which in the East tend to collect round any figure of outstanding holiness. He was horrified. Vermin was one thing, but constant adulation was more than he could bear. After a few weeks he retired again – this time, taking no chances, to the top of a pillar.

Meanwhile the fame of Athos was spreading fast. Before the end of the ninth century there seem to have been several *lavras* already in existence, and in close enough association to stand up for their rights. Another friend of Euthymius, one John Kolobos, had recently set up a monastery of his own a little to the north of the peninsula; and on his death the monks of this foundation tried, by means of forged documents, to assert their authority over the hermits of the Mountain proper. They failed. An Athonite delegation was hurriedly assembled and despatched to Constantinople under a certain Andreas (who is described as a "leading quietist") and returned triumphant with a *chrysobul* from the Emperor Leo VI the Wise confirming them in lawful possession of the entire peninsula. Thus, in about A.D. 900, the special status of the Holy Mountain received imperial recognition.

But the hermits were not much longer to enjoy their supremacy. In the middle of the tenth century there appears upon the Byzantine stage the swarthy, stocky and intensely Greek figure of Nicephorus Phocas. The Empire's greatest and most consistently victorious general, liberator of Crete from the Saracen yoke, he was also a man of deep piety and a genuine mystic who, at his moments of greatest triumph, dreamed only of exchanging the clamour of camp and

6
The approach to Chilandar

7
The monks of Esphigmenou

battlefield for the peace of the religious contemplative. These dreams he had long confided to his spiritual adviser, a monk called Athanasius who accompanied him everywhere, and after the success of the Cretan campaign in 961 (which effectively broke Arab sea power in the eastern Mediterranean and earned him the title of "The White Death of the Saracens") he gave Athanasius his share of the plunder with instructions to build, on Athos, a great monastery to which they might both retire in the evening of their lives.

Then two things happened. First Nicephorus, now a grizzled, surly vegetarian in his mid-fifties, fell violently in love with the Empress Theophano, a publican's daughter who, thanks to her beauty, her brains and a pulsating ambition unshackled by the slightest moral scruple, had married the Emperor Romanus II, driving his mother into exile and his five sisters into convents. Next, in 963, Romanus died and Nicephorus was acclaimed Emperor. No sooner was he settled on the throne than, despite the pleadings of his monkish confessors, he married Theophano in the Nea Basilica of Constantinople.

It was some time before the news reached Athos, where Athanasius' monastery was well on the way to completion. The church was finished but for the domes, and around it the monastic buildings were rising fast – concealing, somewhere in their depths, the small cell which had already been reserved for Nicephorus. At once Athanasius hastened to the capital. Bitterly reproaching his old friend for such a betrayal of trust and for his inexcusable marriage to a courtesan who, even if the rumours that she had poisoned her first husband were discounted, nevertheless fully merited her unsavoury reputation, he concluded by telling him that he had lost all interest in Athos and would not be returning. The Emperor fell on his knees, sobbing regrets and excuses. He could not help himself; he still cherished his monastic dreams; one day, when cares of state permitted, he would put away Theophano and join Athanasius on the Holy Mountain, just as he had always promised. Pressing into the old man's hand a *chrysobul* according formal recognition to the new monastery and rendering it free of all but imperial control, he implored him to go back and finish the task he had begun.

Loaded down with all the treasures, precious relics, endowments and privileges with which Nicephorus strove to appease his agonised conscience – including the great jewelled Bible and reliquary of the True Cross which are still among

8
A monk of Esphigmenou wearing the "great habit" appropriate to his rank

the chief glories of the Mountain – Athanasius returned to Athos. But neither he nor the Emperor was to realise their old dream. On the night of December 10–11, 969, Nicephorus was murdered in his bed by Theophano and her tiny but outstandingly handsome lover John Tzimisces, who seized the throne in his place. Athanasius was spared this further shock: soon after his resumption of the building operations, the half-completed dome of the church had collapsed on his head and killed him.

★   ★   ★

But his monastery had been established, and there it still remains, the oldest and largest foundation on Mount Athos – the Grand Lavra. Its name is misleading, for its whole historical importance lies in the fact that this was no loose association of hermits but a properly regulated cenobitic community, governed by its own abbot, self-sufficient and self-contained, infinitely richer and more powerful than anything else on the Mountain. The little lavras were scandalised: to the hermits, this seemed the very thing that many of them had come to Athos to avoid. While Nicephorus was alive there was clearly nothing to be done; but as soon as they heard of his death they sent another delegation to Constantinople to lay their case before Tzimisces and to lodge a formal complaint against the late Athanasius:

> "For he did oppress the Mountain, and did destroy its ancient habits and usages. For he built magnificent buildings, and constructed towers and harbours. . . . He changed the course of streams, and bought pairs of oxen. He cultivated the fields and planted vineyards and produced fruits, and thus he gave a worldly aspect to the Mountain."[6]

In essence, it was the same wail as has been heard on Athos regularly down the centuries whenever any innovation has been suggested. The new Emperor's reaction was firm and sensible. After taking expert advice from the great monastery of Studium in Constantinople, he confirmed the status of Athanasius' foundation, increased its monkish complement from eighty to a hundred and

---

[6] G. SMYRNAKIS, Monk of Esphigmenou. *To Agion Oros*, Athens, 1903, quoted by M. CHOUKAS, *The Black Angels of Athos*, London, 1935.

twenty, and at the same time formally defined the powers of the hitherto unofficial assembly of hermit-leaders which was by now meeting regularly in Karyes. Since, however, the Grand Lavra itself was henceforth to be represented at this assembly, its very size and strength insured its predominance. It could boast, too, a still more unanswerable claim to supremacy. During its construction the Virgin had appeared to Athanasius on a mountain path and, having established her identity by causing him to smite, Moses-like, a nearby rock from which the obedient water gushed, had announced that she herself would assume the perpetual stewardship of the new foundation. This office she still holds, her day-to-day duties being performed by a deacon-deputy.

ILLS 29 & 12

Now that the Lavra had led, others were quick to follow. Before the tenth century was past, two more monasteries, Iveron and Vatopedi, had sprung up along the east coast; during the next hundred years they were joined by many more, eight of which are still in existence; and so the process continued with a gradually rising monastic population, until the fall of Constantinople at last brought it slowly to a standstill. Even then, its own momentum carried it on a little longer; the most recent of the present Ruling Monasteries, Stavronikita, was established as late as 1540, nearly a century after the Empire had ended.

ILLS 30, 13 & 14

For Athos these later Middle Ages were halcyon, as one monastery after another raised its great walls, topped with a high watch-tower of stone, on coast or crag or, like Philotheou or Chilandar, in some wooded fold of the hills. But even this golden expansion knew its moments of crisis, such as the hideous upheaval towards the end of the eleventh century – still a painful memory on the Mountain – when a body of Vlach shepherds, who had obtained leave to keep the monasteries supplied with milk and wool, were caught carrying on an even more profitable business with their wives and daughters. The scandal quickly reached Constantinople, where the Patriarch instituted an immediate purge – only to discover that half the monks, finding the excitement too much for them, had already left with the shepherds. Unfortunately his intervention aroused the wrath of the Emperor, who maintained that Patriarchs had no jurisdiction over Athonite affairs, always till now an imperial prerogative; and the ensuing quarrel continued to exacerbate relations between the twin authorities for a century to come.

The trouble over the shepherds was not, as might be thought, the origin of
the prohibition of femininity on the Mountain. This uncomfortable tradition
began many centuries before, perhaps when the Empress Pulcheria[7] landed at
some earlier monastery of Vatopedi – that which is said to have commemorated
the site of the bramble-bush under which her father Arcadius had been miraculously washed up after a shipwreck. She was at once turned back by a furious
icon of the Virgin with the words "Go no further; in this place there is another
Queen than thou." The aggressiveness of this pronouncement smacks more of
Hera or Aphrodite than the Mother of God, but a thousand years later the
Panaghia still appears to have felt much the same way; for a similar occurrence
was reported in the fifteenth century when the Princess Mara, daughter of the
Serbian despot George Brancovitch and widow of the Ottoman Sultan
Murad II, attempted to deliver the actual gold, myrrh and frankincense of the
Magi to the monastery of St Paul. She, too, was stopped in her tracks when still
some distance away, and the monks themselves had to carry the precious gifts to
the monastery, where they may still be revered. Another Serbian lady, the wife
of the future Emperor Steven Dushan who accompanied her all-conquering
husband to Mount Athos in 1345, was more successful; so, it must regretfully be
recorded, was Lady Stratford de Redcliffe, British Ambassadress to the Sublime
Porte during the earlier part of the last century. As one of her husband's staff
was subsequently to observe, she ought to have known better. All in all, however, violations have been few – even during Ottoman times, when the Turkish
governors of the Mountain left their harems sadly behind in Stambul, or at any
rate discreetly on the mainland.[8]

And so, apart from the invisible and incorrigible wild life, these hundred and

---

[7] Pulcheria, a strong-minded but unattractive character who had not only vowed perpetual chastity for
herself but had also enforced similar undertakings on her two younger sisters, was the daughter of the
Emperor Arcadius (395–408) and sister of Theodosius II (408–50) for whom she had long acted as Regent and
whom she always dominated. She eventually became the wife, though in name only, of the Emperor Martian
(450–57). She devoted her life to the propagation of Orthodoxy, was largely responsible for the Council of
Chalcedon in 451 and was finally canonised. Other versions of the Athos story connect it with Pulcheria's
aunt, Galla Placidia, famous for the mausoleum at Ravenna where she is buried.

[8] There is, so far as I know, only one piece of first-hand feminine reportage on Athos. A gushing French lady
journalist with a *penchant* for the sensational spent a month there in 1929 disguised as a man, having first
caused her breasts to be amputated in a desperate attempt at virisimilitude. See M. CHOISY, *Un été chez les
hommes*, Paris, 1929.

9
The Abbot of Esphigmenou
in procession on the Feast
Day

10 (overleaf)
A monk fishing

twenty square miles of sunlit, fertile landscape remain totally devoid of femininity, with the result that the atmosphere of Athos, for all its beauty, seems impregnated with a faintly leaden quality which the appearance of an occasional panicky hen – a concession to good living much deplored by the severer monks – does little to diminish. The phenomenon is particularly notice-

ILL. 25

able in Karyes. In the monasteries it is to be expected; in the largely unin-habited countryside it passes unnoticed. But a village, complete with houses, streets and shops and yet bereft of women or children, is against the natural order and therefore sad. The effect of this constant deprivation of womankind on the permanent inhabitants of Athos will be discussed later; it is variable and hard to assess. The visitor, however, and even the casual visitor, cannot but find it strangely oppressive. One man only of the outside world has earned his little niche in history by reacting in the opposite sense – the Salonica gynaecologist, on the verge of a nervous breakdown from overwork, whom Sir Harry Luke found in 1907 taking a rest cure in the one place in the world where there was no risk of an emergency call.[9]

*　　*　　*

In the year 1204 the Byzantine Empire fell victim to a tragedy second only to that of its ultimate downfall – the treacherous attack by the armies of the so-called Fourth Crusade and their Venetian allies, which set a succession of Frankish thugs on the throne of the Emperors and dealt Constantinople a blow from which it never properly recovered. During the three days and nights of indiscriminate pillage which marked its capture and the far longer period of systematic exploitation which followed, the greatest centre of civilisation in the world was stripped of all it possessed that was beautiful and precious. "Never before," wrote Geoffrey of Villehardouin, himself one of the leaders of the Crusade and an eye-witness of what took place, "never before since the creation of the world has such a vast quantity of booty been taken from one city." Nicetas Choniates, a senior Byzantine civil servant regarded in highest esteem, went even further. In comparison to these creatures, he wrote, "who bear

9 Sir HARRY LUKE, "A Thousand Years of Mt Athos", *Cornhill Magazine*, Summer, 1963.

the Cross of Christ on their shoulders, even the Saracens are merciful and kind".[10]

The monasteries trembled. Mount Athos was now part of the new Frankish Kingdom of Salonica and was well known to possess treasures second only to those of Constantinople itself. Fortunately the Marquis Boniface of Montferrat, to whom the kingdom had been allotted, proved slower off the mark than the Emperor Baldwin; before he could give the Mountain his full attention he found that its continued autonomy had been guaranteed by the Pope. For the monks, this was quite bad enough. The Greek and Roman churches had been in schism for a hundred and fifty years and relations between them severely strained for at least twice that period. All Popes, therefore, were anathema; and to have to accept the authority of a papal legate sent by the worldly, autocratic, ever-interfering Innocent III proved an exercise in self-abasement which even the most ascetic were hard put to endure. But worse was to come. When, in 1261, the Latin Empire was overthrown and Michael VIII Palaeologus returned in triumph to his Constantinople, he found the position of his debilitated Empire precarious in the extreme; if it was to survive at all, some accommodation would have to be reached with the West. In the next few years the situation deteriorated still further, while away in Naples Charles of Anjou was preparing an immense expedition against him which Michael knew he could not hope to withstand. Only the Pope could save him now. Gregory X's terms were hard, but the desperate Emperor had no choice. After long argument he managed to persuade a section of the Greek clergy – though not the Patriarch – to accept the inevitable; and so it was that on July 6, 1274, at Lyons, high plenipotentiaries of the Byzantine Empire and Church made formal acknowledgement of the Catholic faith and the supremacy of the Pope of Rome. Technically at least, the Great Schism was over.

The uproar which ensued in Constantinople nearly lost Michael his throne and was quelled only at the cost of appalling persecutions. Athos too, always the focus of reaction, received the news with undisguised horror. Before long the imperial inquisitors appeared on the Mountain. They did their work conscientiously and well, as did the executioners who followed them; but divine

[10] Quoted by G. OSTROGORSKY, *History of the Byzantine State* (translated by J. M. HUSSEY), Oxford, 1956.

displeasure at these outrages was soon made manifest. When, three years after the Council of Lyons, the Emperor's new and more amenable Patriarch Beccus visited the Lavra, the cypresses in front of the church withered as he passed, and the wells ran dry; during the Latin Mass which followed, the entire monastery was shrouded in a black mist. Seven hundred years later, at Karyes and Zographou, the burial-places of the Athonite martyrs are daily revered; throughout the Mountain, the names of Michael Palaeologus and John Beccus are abhorred; while in some secret cave near the Lavra, the bodies of those monks who participated in the dreadful Mass lie uncorrupted – a concept justly repugnant to the Orthodox mind – with their hair, beards and fingernails still growing.

★   ★   ★

For the peace of the Holy Mountain, the beginning of the fourteenth century proved even more disastrous than that of the thirteenth. In 1303 Andronicus II Palaeologus, reduced to hiring mercenaries to defend his Empire against the Turks, enlisted the services of the Grand Company of Catalans – one of those armies of footloose freebooters who were at that time roaming Europe selling their swords to the highest bidder. They saved the immediate situation, but Andronicus was soon to learn what many other rulers before and since have discovered to their cost – that foreign armies summoned in an emergency are often very much harder to get rid of than they are to bring in. The Catalans now turned their vastly superior strength against the Empire itself, terrorising one district after another with systematic raids of pillage and devastation which the Emperor was powerless to prevent. In 1305, after the assassination of their leader in the imperial palace, they abandoned these raids in favour of open warfare, and two years later the full force of Catalan fury was unleashed on Athos. There were now an estimated three hundred religious institutions of one kind or another on the Mountain; within the space of a few months all but the largest and best-defended had been destroyed. Their monks, a contemporary chronicler tells us, were "slaughtered like lambs".

When, in the spring of 1308, this monstrous horde swept off southwards to ravage the Frankish states of Greece, the surviving monasteries were faced with a long period of reconstruction, and it was at about this time that a new and most unexpected phenomenon made its appearance among them – the idiorrhythmic way of life, which wrought complete social revolution to all those houses in which it was adopted and has, ever since, profoundly influenced the development of the entire community. Just how it was introduced remains uncertain, but once established it spread with a most un-Athonite speed. In its essence, the new system is simple enough to describe; to understand its full impact, however, we must look for a moment at the pattern of monastic life as it had hitherto been known in the Orthodox world.

The Eastern Church recognises no distinction of religious orders of the kind familiar in the West. Thus all Orthodox monasticism is based on the pattern established in the fourth century when, in the belief that the eremitic example as set by St Anthony was inconsistent with the ideal of brotherly love, St Pachomius founded and St Basil shaped the earliest Christian cenobitic communities. Despite their efforts, however, succeeding generations of monks proved incapable of steering a middle course between the contrary attractions of a demoralising self-indulgence and an exaggerated, semi-hysterical asceticism. It was thus left to Theodore, Abbot of Studium at the beginning of the ninth century, to codify a monastic way of life which, though rigid enough to preserve discipline, was yet sufficiently flexible to allow for some degree of human weakness and individuality. The so-called Studite Rule which he developed was in its essentials similar to that introduced to the West by St Benedict three hundred years earlier on the basis of poverty, chastity and obedience. It was widely accepted throughout the Orthodox world, had been adopted with minor modifications by Athanasius for the Lavra and had since become standard through all the monasteries of the Mountain.

Then came the idiorrhythmic explosion. The principle on which it was based is impossible to defend on theoretical grounds, since it allows not only the personal possession of wealth but even its manipulation for financial gain. It therefore makes nonsense of the vow of poverty which has always been – and still is, everywhere else – a cornerstone of monastic ideals. In practice, however, the system has proved popular and successful, to the extent that, out of the twenty Ruling Monasteries on Mount Athos, it has been adopted by no less than nine; and more might have followed had the Holy Synod at Karyes not brought the

12
The courtyard of Vatopedi

trend firmly to a stop. Today, any further lapses by cenobitic monasteries into idiorrhythmy are forbidden, though the idiorrhythmics are always at liberty to revert to their former way of life.[11] Such success is surprising; so liberal a principle might well have caused these monasteries, deprived of much of their cohesive force, to disintegrate altogether. Once, however, it had proved itself in practice, its popularity was to be expected – since, for an idiorrhythmic monk, life is very largely what he chooses to make it. With such money as he possesses after payment of his entrance fee, supplemented if need be by wages paid for his monastic work, he buys his food, his clothes and other small necessities. Later, when he has attained some seniority in the monastery and if he has the money and inclination, he may exchange his cell for less austere accommodation: in the more prosperous monasteries, nearly all of them idiorrhythmic, it is quite common for an elder to occupy an extremely well-appointed bed-sitter or even a suite of two or three communicating rooms, each with its private balcony. Here he will read, sleep, work if necessary, and spend his abundant leisure. Here, too, he will eat the meals he has prepared – unless, as is still sometimes the case, he has a young acolyte-servant to do his cooking; for the refectories of the idiorrhythmic houses have lain disused for hundreds of years except on the great feast-days of the Church. His daily life is, in fact, inescapably reminiscent of that led by the more crusted bachelor dons in Oxford and Cambridge colleges – except perhaps that the latter are apt to spend rather less of their time at worship. But even regular attendance at services, though usual, is not altogether obligatory in the idiorrhythmic monasteries, and the observer is left wondering whether the monkish vocation is after all wholly incompatible with a life of ease.

ILL. 22

Conclusions of this kind can, however, be misleading. These monasteries are not just permanent rest homes for idle celibates, nor are they normally treated as such. The apparent laxity of their rule, in fact, allows scope for individuals to practise an austerity neither possible nor permissible under the alternative régime. It also attracts the more educated type of monk, able and perhaps eager to think for himself, to whom the Borstal-like disciplines of the cenobitic houses

---

[11] No idiorrhythmic monastery has in fact ever reverted to cenobitic system. The Serbian monastery of Chilandar wished to do so in 1933; but since one of its conditions was that the Abbot should be appointed by the Serbian hierarchy, the Holy Synod – always fearful of foreign political influence – refused.

might soon become unbearable. Finally, it is preferred by most young ecclesiastics aspiring to promotion. There is a rule of the Orthodox Church which requires that its upper hierarchy should be drawn from the monasteries rather than from the priesthood; and the ambitious novice usually finds an idiorrhythmic house on Athos a more congenial milieu than any other for his monastical apprenticeship.

The other fundamental difference between the two systems lies in the form of monastic government adopted by each. The cenobitic houses are virtual dictatorships, subject to the complete control of their abbot, who is elected for life. In 1406 a *typicon* issued by Manuel II Palaeologus placed this election in the hands of the fifteen most distinguished monks of the monastery, the *epitropoi*, since, he wrote,

"The cities that are well-managed are governed by the will of the best and not of the many, nor of the first comers, nor even the will of the ruler alone; for the one is democracy, the other tyranny – both equally outlandish."

But despite these enlightened words, the Emperor could do nothing to curb the power of an abbot once elected. Though the *epitropoi* may give him help and advice, the final decisions remain his and his alone, and the universal vow of obedience ensures that they are properly observed.

So autocratic a rule is rejected by the idiorrhythmic monasteries, who have accordingly done away with abbots altogether, substituting a committee of three *epitropoi*, elected by the senior monks for one year only and backed by a permanent council of elders. As a system of government it is, undeniably, less picturesque; the spectacle of an abbot in full sail, billowing in awful solemnity from *katholikon*[12] to refectory, and there, having ponderously laid aside the gleaming staff of his office, being nudged into position behind his individual high table until he at last comes safely to berth in the great carved throne reserved for his use, is an experience that leaves the beholder permanently enriched; and the absence of such splendour from the idiorrythmic monasteries diminishes them in proportion. But the average idiorrhythmic monk considers

[12] The central church of the monastery.

such sacrifices a small price to pay for the advantages he enjoys. On occasion, if he has any ability, he will find himself in a position of considerable power within his own monastery; and at all times he will be guaranteed a degree of liberty unknown to his cenobitic brothers, preserved alike from the rigours of their rule and the tyranny of domineering abbots. An elder of Xeropotamou expressed it best when I asked him why he preferred the idiorrhythmic system. "This way," he said, "we feel safer."

★   ★   ★

The twenty Ruling Monasteries – one Serbian, one Russian, one Bulgarian and seventeen Greek – are supreme on Athos. They are the nuclei around which the life of the community revolves, the sole sources from which it derives its waning strength. They alone are permitted to own land; they alone are represented, each by a single member, on the Holy Synod at Karyes, the Athonite parliament which can dispute with those of Iceland and the Isle of Man the honour of being the oldest administrative assembly in the world. But territorial affluence and political power are not everything, least of all in the rarefied atmosphere of the Mountain; and for those who find themselves unsuited to life within a Ruling Monastery an alternative is open. Like so many past generations of English misfits, they can always escape to the colonies.

Athonite colonies, which tend to group themselves round the southern end of the peninsula, are many and various. First in size and seniority come the dozen or so *sketes*. Several of these, in particular the hulking Russian abominations of St Elias and St Andrew, are as big as if not bigger than their mother-monasteries, though they are now apt to be populated by only a handful of monks, far advanced in senility. Except that they are governed by a deacon rather than an abbot, and that their central place of worship is known, not as a *katholikon* but as a *kyriakon* (from which the Scottish *kirk* and our own word *church* is derived), the cenobitic sketes are practically indistinguishable in organisation from cenobitic monasteries. On the other hand, they are nearly always a good deal poorer and – by necessity as well as by inclination – more ascetic. Nor are they supposed to own domestic animals.

Whereas monasteries have become idiorrhythmic as a result of a relaxation of their rule, the idiorrhythmic sketes owe their character to a contrary process, having developed from purely haphazard associations of scattered hermitages. The skete of St Anne, therefore, or that of Kapsokalyvia,[13] bears no resemblance at all to a monastery but looks like a small village, with a few whitewashed cottages clustered round a central church. Life there is austere; but it is un-expectedly infused, more than anywhere else on Athos outside Karyes, by the spirit of private enterprise – for the monks of the idiorrhythmic sketes are the artisans of the Mountain. Here are the carpenters and the masons, the wood-carvers and the fresco-painters, all willing and eager to accept commissions. From the artistic point of view their standards are distressingly low – Byzantine *bondieuserie* can be every whit as wounding to the spirit as the most merciless perpetrations of Lisieux or Lourdes – but, to many an Orthodox community beyond the seas, an icon painted on the Holy Mountain possesses a *cachet* far outweighing any uncertainties of taste or weakness of execution. And so, in the name of the Lord, the grim work goes on.

Dotted all over the peninsula, in the fields, forests and clearings, some perched precariously on the hillsides, others more sedately settled along the coastal strand, lie the *kellia*. When isolated, they are immediately recognisable – small cottages, roofed with wood or wattle, each surrounded by its kitchen garden neatly sown with bean and tomato, cucumber and lettuce. Grouped together, they could easily be mistaken for an idiorrhythmic skete but for the fact that they have no central church; every *kelli*, being quite independent of its neighbours and responsible only to the Ruling Monastery to which it belongs, possesses its own individual chapel. It is occupied, as a rule, by from two to four monks – usually gardeners, since, just as the sketes are predominantly artisan, so the kellia are agricultural. These monks, arguably among the freest on Athos, are almost certainly the best-fed, since they can not only enjoy their own garden produce but are also permitted to keep any male animals which they may care to import

---

[13] Kapsokalyvia means literally "the burnt huts". The name commemorates a celebrated ascetic of the fourteenth century, Maximos, whose habit it was regularly to burn down his hut lest, by occupying it for too long, he might start feeling comfortable. He also possessed the gift of levitation, and frequently flew to the top of the Mountain for conversations with the Virgin. He was well known as a prophet and is said to have foretold to the Emperor John VI Cantacuzene that he would end his life as a monk. (The Emperor did, and is said to be buried in the narthex of Vatopedi.)

14
Chilandar

from the mainland. Theirs, too, are the indefensible hens – still in evidence despite that Herodian edict by which, in 1932, the Holy Synod ordered the immediate massacre of the entire chicken population of the Mountain. Faced with such comparative abundance, one is tempted to suspect here a rather less drastic system of fasting than that followed in the sketes and monasteries: and indeed, since the kelliots have no superior to direct their lives, the degree of ascetism which they pursue and even the amount of time they spend at their devotions, is entirely their own affair. No wonder they seem so contented.

Last, the hermits. The Orthodox Church has always, despite the strictures of St Basil, kept a place for those who feel the need of perpetual solitude. Monasteries, *sketes* and *kellia* may come and go, but the earliest and most primitive form of religious settlement on the Mountain has never, in perhaps fifteen centuries, lost its hold; and there, at the very tip of the promontory where the

ILL. 54

southern wall of Athos plunges near-perpendicular to the sea, are the caves and eyries that shelter the spiritual heirs of Peter and Euthymius and all their nameless, numberless predecessors. These are the real ascetics; and their chosen places of retreat are well suited to their purpose. Here the green fertility of the rest of the peninsula gives way to a world of barren rock, defenceless alike against sun and storm and the unrelenting, salt-laden wind. Here is the desert of Athos, and hither the hermits come.

Not all of them demand complete isolation. The wattle huts, no larger than a garden shed, that lean out so perilously from imperceptible ledges perhaps five or six hundred feet up the cliff-face, may hold two or three of these men, living out their lives in such merciless proximity to one another as to constitute in itself a form of fleshly mortification. Most of their time is spent in prayer. Only occasionally may they be seen, slipping and stumbling over the rocks, gathering the leaves, berries and occasional figs which form their principal diet, or descending as best they can to the landing-stage to meet the *caïque* whose regular calls, when the sea allows, provide their only link with the rest of the Mountain.

Such hermits, confined to a few square yards of unyielding mountainside and subjected, while in a chronic state of near-starvation, to remorseless extremes of heat and cold, endure an austerity beyond the power of most mortals to conceive; but to some of their fellows it is still insufficient. They must go

c

further, to the ultimate in physical and psychological endurance, to a lifetime of silence and unbroken solitude; and, if their monastery judges them suitable – for on Athos even hermits must have a monastic affiliation – they will have their wish. Their dwelling may be a windowless hovel, hidden away in some secret place; or they may be allotted a cave in that part of the cliff which rises so sheer as to defeat any but a skilled climber – one to which the only practicable access is by means of ropes and pulleys. In the latter case, they must depend for their subsistence entirely on their parent monastery: a monk is despatched at regular intervals to a point above the cave-mouth, whence he lets down a basket of meagre provisions. After a suitable wait he pulls it up again. Only if the basket has not been emptied may he lower himself, if he can, to the cave. Then, if the hermit is found to be dead, his body is removed and a new occupant installed. Later his skull will be returned to the hermitage, to take its place among those of his predecessors on the special shelf reserved for them.

Several of these caves have been continuously inhabited for centuries. The true solitary is often still in his twenties when, adopting some ascetic patron like St Simeon Stylites or St Makarios,[14] he retires from the living world; and on the Holy Mountain, especially in the hermitages, lives are long. Sixty, seventy years in such solitude, with perhaps never the sight of another human being, are not uncommon. And still on Athos, despite its fast-declining population, there are not only the men to occupy these hermitages but others, scarcely more than youths, waiting to succeed them. Many may be already mentally unbalanced; others, sooner or later, will surely become so; but somewhere among them all, unknown and unrecognised, there is, quite possibly, a saint.

*   *   *

No European country that has had to endure a prolonged period of Ottoman rule has ever fully recovered from the experience. Unless deliberately aroused, the Turks were not by nature either cruel or intolerant; and the local governors, once they had ensured a regular flow of supplementary income and such other

---

[14] It was the distinction of St Makarios to have suffered such remorse at having squashed a mosquito which was in the act of biting him that he at once retired to the nearby bog that was the insects' principal breeding-ground. There he remained, naked, for six months. On his return he was so covered with suppurating boils that his friends could recognise him only by his voice.

items as might be necessary for their rather primitive pleasures, were usually content to sit back and enjoy them. But the atmosphere of indolence and corruption which this attitude engendered proved in the long run far more injurious than any persecution. Its effect was like a shot of anaesthetic; the subject peoples were left intellectually paralysed, with the result that for four or five centuries much of eastern Europe became a cultural desert. Fallow lay the fields of secular painting and of sculpture, of literature and of music; and it is today almost impossible to find, anywhere in this immense area, a single non-religious building of the slightest architectural merit constructed during the years of Turkish occupation.

In this dark and spiritless time, one single organisation remained capable of keeping alive such cultural embers as had not been entirely extinguished. The Orthodox Church, always a powerful political force since the early days of the Empire, became the only means, apart from language, by which the various national elements within its flock could preserve their identities, and the last existing focus for both past tradition and future aspiration. That this function is not even now entirely dead has been amply demonstrated by the recent history of Cyprus, where Archbishop Makarios continues to furnish a superb example of the Byzantine conception of churchmanship. In Ottoman times it was paramount; and churches and monasteries throughout the Turkish dominions were acutely conscious of a mission in which, worldly as it might appear, they did not fail to discern the will of God.

Nowhere in the Orthodox world was this consciousness more intensely real than on Mount Athos, uniquely suited by reason of its continued autonomy to preserve the holy heritage of Byzantium unimpaired. Until the first Greek insurrection against the Turks in 1821 it was recognised as the supreme centre of Hellenistic thought; and even after the establishment, far to the south, of the embryonic Greek kingdom eight years later, it retained its prestige as a nationalist-religious hearth, the forcing-ground *par excellence* of bishops and patriarchs and their ultimate refuge when, as quite often happened, they incurred the Sultan's disfavour. Yet only once in the whole history of Ottoman–Athonite relations was this disfavour extended to the Mountain itself. This was during the 1821 troubles when the monks, having unwisely advertised their support for the insurgents, found three thousand Turkish soldiers billeted on them to re-establish their former loyalties. Fortunately for all parties, the soldiers did not find it necessary to stay long; on their arrival, five thousand out of the total monastic population of six thousand fled in terror to the mainland.

With this exception, the four hundred and eighty-two years during which the Holy Mountain lay under Ottoman domination were generally uneventful. The great days of expansion were over; after the fall of the Empire, there was neither the money nor the incentive for much further building. So it was that the monks confined their activities to the field of ideas and – ostensibly at any rate – gave the Turks no trouble; while the latter, for their part, continued to show a religious tolerance which many of their Christian contemporaries in western Europe would have done well to emulate. There were, admittedly, certain exceptions to this rule; the Sultan Selim I, for example, who reigned from 1512 to 1520 and in those eight years liquidated some forty thousand Islamic heretics of the Shia persuasion, was – if we may believe the Encyclopaedia Britannica – "with difficulty dissuaded from ordering the complete extirpation of all the Christians in Turkey". But whether it was the sheer magnitude of the task that put him off – at that time it would have meant the depopulation of the whole Balkan peninsula – or whether it was the same natural reluctance to cause suffering that had earlier led him to abolish the practice of roasting criminals before a slow fire, the Sultan once again gave confirmation to the old truism that, whenever religious persecution is in the air, it is safer to be a heathen than a heretic; and on the Mountain, where he is said to have restored and re-endowed the monastery of Xeropotamou and commanded that its lamps should be supplied with oil in perpetuity by the Ottoman Court, his name is actually revered.

The services, then, that the monasteries of Athos were able to render to the cause of Hellenism were made possible only by the surprising degree of tolera-tion – and occasional active sympathy – shown towards them by the Turkish authorities. But their contribution, for all its importance, was nationalist rather than strictly intellectual. Nothing could be more misleading than to compare it with the work of the great Latin monasteries which, throughout the dark ages, kept the spark of academic endeavour alive in the West. The Orthodox

16
Fresco illustrating the Akáthistos Hymn, line 217, "The garrulous Rhetors became as dumb as fishes before thee, O Mother of God"

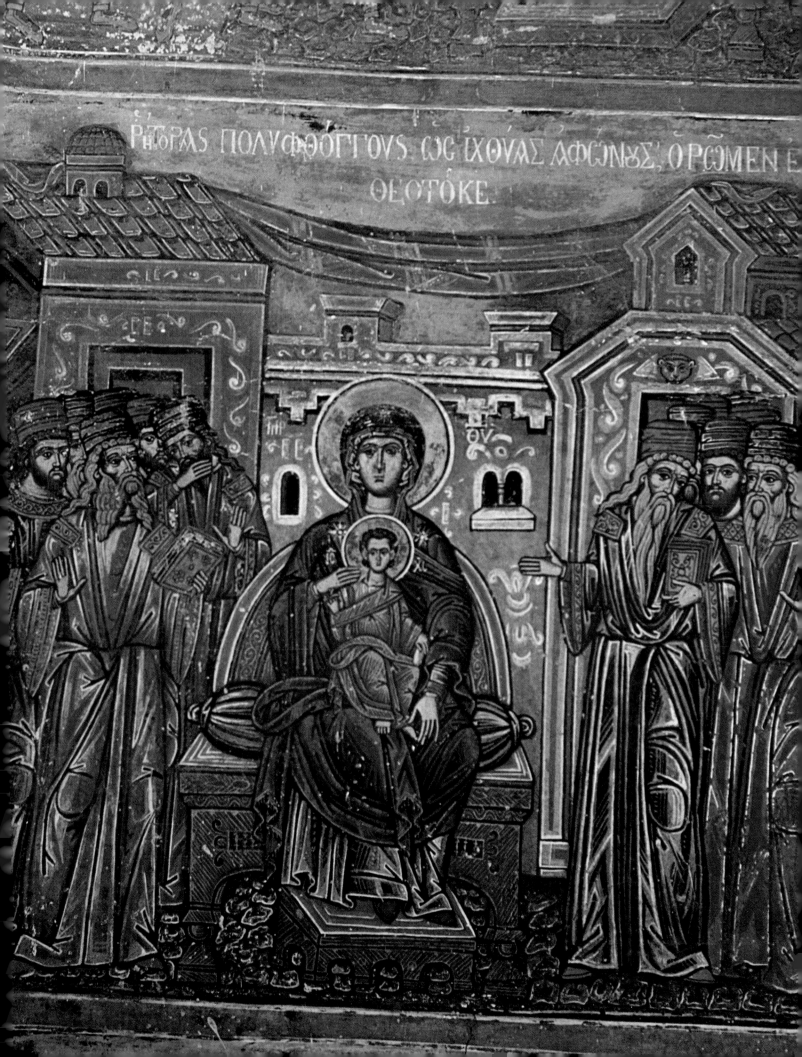

ΡΗΤΟΡΑΣ ΠΟΛΥΦΘΟΓΓΟΥΣ ΩΣ ΙΧΘΥΑΣ ΑΦΩΝΟΥΣ, ΟΡΩΜΕΝ Ε
ΘΕΟΤΟΚΕ

Church, has never performed such a function. During the Byzantine period it did not need to do so, because – unlike the West, where normal cultural life took the best part of a thousand years to recover from the transfer of the capital to Constantinople and from the barbarian invasions that followed – the Eastern Empire was blessed with a continuous secular intellectual tradition; most learned Byzantine monks acquired their knowledge before, not after, taking the monastic habit. Under the Turkish occupation the monasteries might well have adopted a more consciously academic role; but they were by now set in their ways. That predisposition to mysticism which has always characterised the religious life of the East had permeated them too deeply. Monks who were not mystics or genuine contemplatives were usually patriots, or would-be bishops, or ne'er-do-wells. Few, very few, were scholars.

For, in the Orthodox view, the task of the monk is not so much to study nor to teach, to labour in fields or workshops or scriptoria, not even – except incidentally, if his monastery has money to spare – to occupy himself with good works. He exists in order to pray. In the words of the Emperor Justinian, "the monastic life and its contemplation is a divinely appointed state and it brings souls to God, not only assisting those who profess it but also helping the rest of mankind by reason of its purity and its prayers".[15] Such a life, if diligently pursued over a long period of years, may – we are told – bring divine revelation. It may also, unless carefully supervised, lead to hallucination and hysteria. The difficulty has always been to distinguish the one from the other. Where the case of an individual monk is in question, the problem can usually be settled within his own monastery; but sometimes his ecstasy proves infectious. Then the entire community is shaken and, probably, split; heresy is in the wind; and serious trouble is on its way.

Of this trouble the Holy Mountain has borne its full share. One occasion in particular is worth recording here, since not only did it engender the most desperate theological conflict of the later Byzantine Age but it also provides us with a perfect example of the lengths to which Athonite monks were prepared to be led in their quest for spiritual exaltation. Since the eleventh century there

[15] Justinian, preface to *Novel* No. 133. Quoted by Prof. J. M. HUSSEY, "Byzantine Monasticism" in *History*, June 1939.

had flourished among certain Orthodox divines the belief that the celestial light which had illumined Mount Tabor on the day of the Transfiguration could be re-evoked by a prolonged contemplation of the navel. For the reader wishing to attempt the experiment for himself, the following instructions by a certain Simeon, known as the New Theologian and generally credited with the invention of this doctrine, may be useful:

"When thou art alone in thy cell, shut thy door and seat thyself in a corner: raise thy mind above all things vain and transitory; recline thy beard and chin on thy breast; turn thy eyes and thy thought towards the middle of thy belly, the region of the navel; and search the place of the heart, the seat of the soul. At first all will be dark and comfortless; but if you persevere day and night, you will feel an ineffable joy; and no sooner has the soul discovered the place of the heart, than it is involved in a mystic and etherial light."[16]

This curious technique became an important feature of the so-called Hesychast movement, which was introduced on to Athos by its founder, Gregory of Sinai, in the early fourteenth century. It seems, moreover, to have yielded highly satisfactory rewards, for by 1341 a cultivated if somewhat embittered Greek monk from Calabria named Barlaam found the Mountain rife with its practitioners. An Aristotelian rationalist, formed in the scholastic traditions of the West, Barlaam was profoundly shocked by what he saw, and immediately denounced the Hesychasts as blasphemers and heretics. The resulting controversy, combined with a political crisis which soon led to civil war, split the Empire for a decade, and it was not until 1351 that the victorious new Emperor, John VI Cantacuzene, was able to preside over a council in Constantinople which effectively upheld the Hesychast cause. Thus, the omphalopsychic light that Gibbon was to stigmatise three centuries later as "the production of a distempered fancy, the creature of an empty stomach and an empty brain" was finally established as the same true manifestation of the divine energy as had appeared to the disciples on Mount Tabor; Barlaam and his followers were excommunicated. Nor has their

[16] Quoted by GIBBON, *Decline and Fall of the Roman Empire*, Chapter LVIII.

offence been forgiven. On the Sunday of Orthodoxy, when it is the custom of the Eastern Church to read out the names of those anathematised for heresy, that of Barlaam of Calabria still heads the list.

* * *

Other, less awkward, aspects of Hesychasm – the discipline for example, of perpetual prayer, with the name of Jesus continually repeated, coordinated with the respiration and heartbeat – have been known since the beginnings of the Christian era and are still practised on Athos by those of sufficient training; and indeed any Athonite monk, however modest his spiritual attainments, must expect to spend the great part of his waking life in prayer. Three times in every twenty-four hours he is summoned to his devotions by the clatter of the ILL. 58 *semandron* – that great plank of wood, scarred and seasoned by long centuries of use, which serves each monastery in place of a bell and reverberates with the most characteristic and immediately evocative of all the noises of the Mountain. Like so much else on Athos, this noise is itself symbolic. The katholikon, standing free by invariable tradition in the middle of the courtyard, represents the ark of salvation; and the monk who walks around it three times, balancing the semandron on his shoulder and rapping it with a little wooden hammer in urgent tattoo, is in fact echoing the sound of Noah's tools summoning the chosen to join him while time yet remains. His first circuit is a call to reptiles and creeping things; his second is for all four-footed creatures; his last, for the sons of men.

Throughout Athos the working – or, more properly, the praying – day starts soon after midnight, when the monasteries are roused from their slumber for the first, longest and most important of the daily services. This lasts till dawn and is followed by a meal, after which come a few hours for sleep, work or private prayer. In the early afternoon the semandron is heard again, its sharp staccato rhythm sometimes falling to the very brink of audibility before it rises again in a swift *crescendo* and the whole monastery seems to vibrate with its challenge. This time the call is for vespers, which occupy roughly another three hours. Then there normally comes another, lighter, meal, preparatory to that period of mauve contentment when the monks repair to the balconies and belvederes that are such a constantly beguiling feature of Athonite domestic architecture. There, on clear summer evenings, those whose monasteries lie on the west of the peninsula may wait while the sun, blazing its path across the sea, gently sinks behind the distant ridge of Longos, while those on the east will gaze upon the high peak of the Holy Mountain itself as it turns from grey to pink to purple, its shadow speeding across the Aegean till it merges with the little streak of cloud that marks, on the furthest horizon, the hills of Samothrace. There, too, while a glass of home-distilled *ouzo* warms them with its soft enthusiasm, the more worldly will discuss the one topic which, even on Athos, can hold its own with theology and monastic affairs as a never-failing stimulus to conversation – politics. For you may deprive a Greek monk of his family and his friends, of the company of all womankind, of most of his food and much of his sleep, and he will make no protest; but if you take from him his politics – then, unless he is very, very close to God, he will surely die.

The sun sets, and the air sharpens; and before long the semandron is calling the monastery back to work. Evening compline is short – little more than an hour – and so the monks retire to their cells to snatch what sleep they can before the whole cycle begins afresh. It is not entirely unvarying. Some fifty times a year there is an *agrypnia* – an all-night service of vigil that continues without a break for a full twelve hours – and the great annual feasts of the Church are punctiliously observed with such ceremony as tradition may dictate. Once a year, too, each monastery celebrates its own individual feast when, after several days of frenzied preparation, official guests from neighbouring houses and any other travellers who may be passing are bidden to join the brothers in the refectory for a meal – an experience from which, if they are strangers to the Mountain, they will not immediately recover.

But feasts on Mount Athos are much less frequent than fasts; and the amount of food consumed per head must be the lowest in Europe. For a start, all the monasteries fast for two months before Easter, a month following Whitsun, a fortnight before the Dormition, another fortnight before the feast of St Peter and St Paul, and forty days before Christmas. To these prolonged periods must be added a considerable number of day-long fasts in honour of various saints; and we are left with the sobering conclusion that Athonite monks subsist, for at

18
Reliquary of the True Cross displayed at Vatopedi

19 (overleaf)
Roumanian monk near Xeropotamou with Longos in the distance

least five months a year, at little above starvation level. Moreover, even during the remainder of the year in the cenobitic monasteries, one meal only is provided on Mondays, Wednesdays and Fridays. It is served at noon, and may contain no cheese, butter or oil. In these monasteries eggs and fresh fish (apart from shell-fish and octopus) are reserved for feast-days only; meat is never seen at all. The idiorrhythmics do slightly better, for here the monks eat in their own quarters and can therefore do so as frequently as they wish; but they, too, keep Wednesdays and Fridays as lean days. At other times they may eat meat, but they do so very rarely; it is expensive (since hunting on the Mountain is forbidden by Canon Law), invariably tough, and – in theory at any rate – may not be prepared in monastic kitchens.

Such austerity has not been an invariable rule. The first known English visitor to Mount Athos, Dr John Covel, later Master of Christ's College, Cambridge, wrote rapturously of the delicacies offered to him at the Lavra in 1677: ". . . the best monkish fare that could be gotten was provided, excellent fish (severall ways), oyl, salet, beanes, hortechokes, beets, chees, onions, garlick, olives, caveor, Pyes of herbs, φακαίς, κτωπόδι, pepper, salt and saffron in all. At last conserved little oranges, most exquisite, good wine (a sort of small claret) and we alwayes drank most plentifully. . . . He is no Greek that cannot drink twenty or thirty plump glasses at a setting." Covel, be it said, was a man of adventurous palate, a fact which he proved at Vatopedi where "they gave us Limpets thrice as big as oures in England and yellow, all cover'd with a fat yellow mosse which they eat either alone or with oil; and tast well".[17] A Dr Hunt, who early in the last century was invited to dine with Gregorios V, the exiled Patriarch of Constantinople, fared better still. "The hour of dinner was 9 o'clock in the morning; we found his table furnished in a style quite unconventual, with lamb, sausages, hams and French wines. His dispensing power seems to remain although he is dethroned; and seven or eight of the salad-fed monks who dined with us appeared to be much pleased with their change of diet. . . . His conversation seemed to indicate that he looked forward to be reinstated in his honours."[18]

[17] J. COVEL, *The Journal of John Covel*, with notes by F. W. HASLUCK, in the Annual of the British School at Athens (*The First English Traveller's Account of Athos*), Vol. XVIII, pp. 103–31.
[18] M. A. HUNT, from the papers of Dr Hunt; No. IX, pp. 198–232, in *Memoirs Relating to European and Asiatic Turkey*, edited by ROBERT WALPOLE, 1817.

20
An Elder of Esphigmenou
in his cell

Gregorios did in fact return soon afterwards to Constantinople – but not for long. In the spring of 1821 news of the Greek rising reached the Porte; on Easter morning, by order of the Sultan, he was publicly hanged over the main gate of his Patriarchate and a massacre of thirty thousand Greeks followed. But that is a story that does not concern us here. Rather let us return to Athonite food, a subject of inexhaustible fascination on which scarcely any writer with first-hand experience of the Holy Mountain has forborne to comment. Few of these comments, it must be said, have been as favourable as those quoted above; and today there can be no question about it – any visit to Athos spells gastronomic martyrdom. For the first few meals, while courage and self-discipline remain steady, a person of normal digestive sensibility may be able to contemplate – and even, in part, consume – the interminable platefuls of beans, spasmodically enlivened by a single slice of anchovy or a slab of briny cheese, which, if the monasteries had their way, would stand alone between himself and starvation. But on such a diet the spirit soon flags. Within a day or two those liverish-white lumps, glaring remorselessly up at him from their puddle of stone-cold grease, take on a new expression, hostile and challenging. "Bet you can't," they seem to say. And they are right.

Thus, even more than its inexpressible nastiness, it is the uniformity of the monastic menu that wears one down. The memory gratefully cherishes an omelette at Karakallou; Lavra noodles; and once, at Chilandar, a perfectly splendid fish. It also returns to an evening at Dionysiou on my first visit, when we caught an octopus and were promised it for breakfast. Alas, we were disappointed; it was hung up for the night, like an apron, behind the kitchen door and the cat had got most of it by morning. But these occasions are exceptional. Over all normal meals those unrelenting beans will continue to cast their baleful spell; and the visitor will feel more and more like a refractory child who, having refused its lunch, finds itself confronted with the same grim offering, congealed, at supper. Now at last he will fully appreciate the old custom of cenobitic monasteries according to which, as the monks pass out of the refectory, the cooks ask pardon on their knees for the atrociousness of the meal;[19] now,

[19] I have not been able to confirm whether this custom is anywhere still observed. It was reported by Dimitrakopoulos in 1896, and is quoted by DAWKINS, *The Monks of Athos*, London, 1936.

too, he will begin to understand why, among all the ascetic disciplines of the Mountain, that of almost continuous fasting is so insistently stressed.

This increasing wisdom, however, will be offset by the appearance of a curious new disorientation regarding the passage of time. Time is always a problem on Athos. First of all, as everyone knows, it goes more slowly; but the problem is more complicated than this. Not content with the Julian calendar – which now runs thirteen days behind our normal Gregorian one and in 1962 allowed me to celebrate my birthday on two separate occasions – all the monasteries except Vatopedi and Iveron (which has an equally impossible system of its own)[20] still cling doggedly to Byzantine time. Their day begins at sunset, which thus becomes twelve o'clock. In consequence, those Athonite clocks with any pretensions to accuracy are apt to give the impression of being anything between five and eight hours slow, the degree of apparent error varying with the inexorable march of the seasons. Admittedly such clocks are rare, since the necessity of regulating them daily causes the large majority to collapse under the strain; but to the unaccustomed eye the breakdown of a Byzantine timepiece can long pass undetected.

Deprived, then, of any artificial system of time measurement, one instinctively falls back on the natural guide – the stomach – only to find oneself foiled again. In normal life the concepts of "morning" and "afternoon" are neatly separated by the mid-day meal; not, however, on Athos. Here the visitor can usually expect to be fed an hour or so after his arrival at a monastery, which itself may occur at any time of day; he may have been walking, or riding, for two hours or for eight; he may be still suffering the after-effects of the coffee, *ouzo* and immense cube of Turkish delight which constitute many an Athonite breakfast, or he may be ravenously hungry – at least till the food appears. Then, faced with yet another plate of beans, he will find nothing to help him identify it as lunch or dinner; while even the beans themselves, in their evocation of so many similar

[20] Iveron, true to its origins, still sticks to the old Georgian system of time measurement by which, according to a tradition said to be inherited from the Zoroastrians, twelve o'clock is adjusted to the hour of sunrise. Vatopedi, on the other hand, has a reputation for keeping up with the times and so follows the general system of the outside world. It has even sought, and received, patriarchal permission to celebrate certain fixed feasts according to the Gregorian calendar – a practice which has brought down upon both it and the Patriarchate the severe opprobrium of its fellow-monasteries.

platefuls in the past, seem imbued with a strangely timeless quality. What, then, has he left to cling to? All he knows is that the sun is high in the sky and that the gigantic grandfather clock in the corner of the room – of nineteenth-century Croydon manufacture – is ticking ponderously on, with its hands pointing to twenty minutes past seven. Suddenly, the bottom seems to have fallen out of his world.

* * *

Such anxieties as these do not trouble the monks. Their day may be regulated by the semandron, but their life knows nothing of time. Nor is it desirable that it should. Life, for them, is merely a purgatorial preliminary to death, which will at last unite the soul with God. It should therefore be approximated to death as much as possible; and just as death is timeless, so should life be also. This accounts for the constant reminders of mortality to be seen everywhere on the Mountain – the ossuaries, for example, or the meticulously preserved monastic collections of skulls, each labelled with the name of the owner and the date of his death; or even the skull-and-crossbones motif on the habit of the *megaloskhimoi*, the monks of the highest grade.

For on Athos, as elsewhere, advancement is possible, though it is based on spiritual, rather than temporal criteria. It has no connection with the priesthood; the lowliest monk may be a priest, but not even one of the highest grade may officiate at services unless he has been properly ordained. This is a ladder of holiness alone. The first stage for any monk is his novitiate, during which he is known as a *rasophoros*, or cassock-wearer. He may, if he chooses, remain in this grade all his life; but more usually, having taken his final vows, he is promoted to the rank of *mikroskhimos*, a man of the Little Habit. For most monks, and particularly those in the idiorrhythmic monasteries who maintain some interest in the outside world, the Little Habit suffices; but a few, with a larger capacity for asceticism and deeper spiritual resources, will go on to adopt the Great and Angelic Habit. These *megaloskhimoi* fast still more rigorously than their fellows; their lives seem to be devoted almost exclusively to prayer and meditation. On normal days they wear no distinguishing dress; only on the great feasts of the Church or before taking Communion do they don the curious

ILL. 57

ILL. 8

21
Detail of the frescoes in the apse of the refectory at Vatopedi

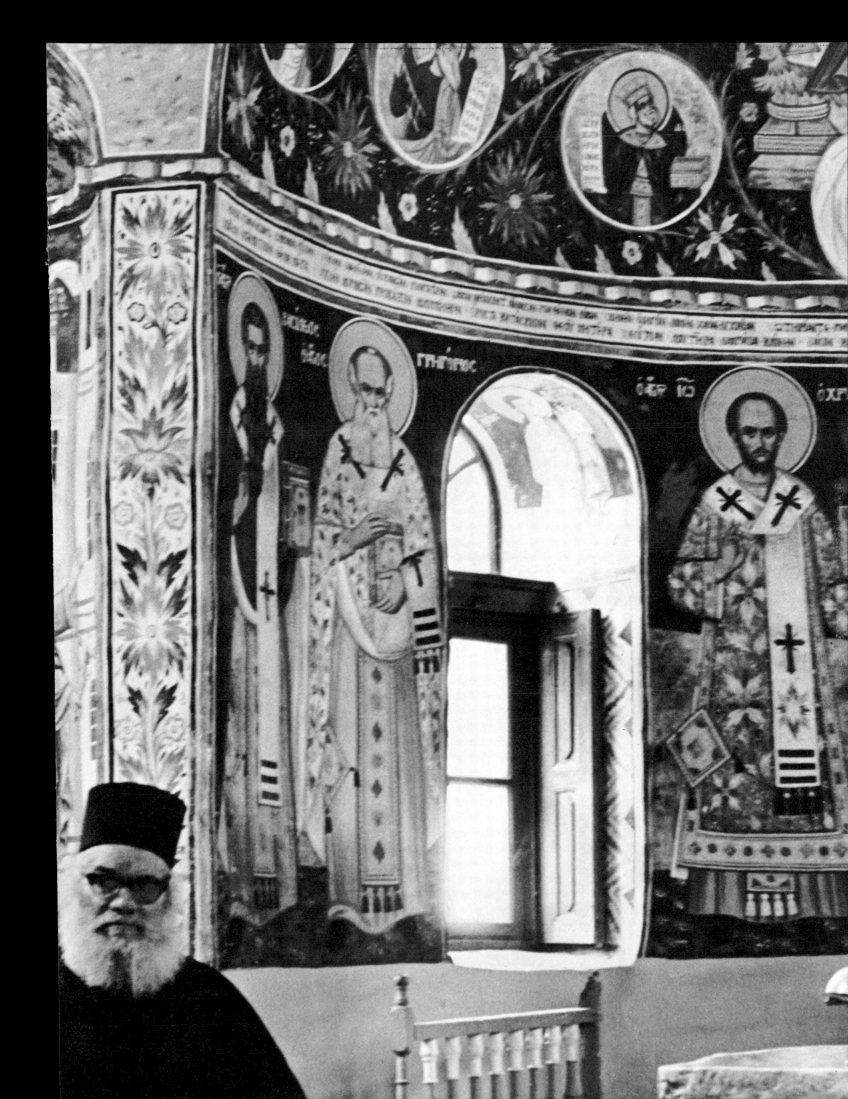

black apron, embroidered with letters and Christian symbols in almost cabbalistic combinations, which proclaims their superior sanctity.

These grades are essential if any true spiritual awareness is to be maintained
in the monasteries; for the monks, despite the regimentation of their life and the
often bewildering uniformity of their outward appearance, differ enormously
in background, character and outlook. A large proportion, perhaps even the
majority, first came to the Mountain in response to a genuine vocation; for
many indeed, who arrived in early adolescence or even before, it is the only
world of which they have any knowledge at all. There is a record of one monk,
a certain Michael Tolotos, whose mother had died at his birth and who was
brought to Athos when only four hours old; he died during the last war at the
age of eighty, never once having seen a woman. For such men as these, the
austerity of Athonite life holds no horrors. They ask only the protection they
have always known, and their fear of the outside world leads them inevitably
to despise it.

But there are others who seek the Holy Mountain for very different reasons.
These are the misfits, the maladjusted, the eternal failures for whom the world
has proved too hostile or too strong. To them Athos offers a freedom from
responsibility which they can find nowhere else. Some have been crossed in
love; others have suffered financial ruin; yet others are labouring under physical
disability; still more have drifted hopelessly from one occupation to another
until at last, middle-aged and disillusioned, they have given up the struggle.
Most travellers on the Mountain will have come across one or more venerable
patriarchs who, on being addressed, reply in fluent English with unmistakable
overtones of the Bronx; a Greek-American sociologist has recorded that of the
five thousand Greek monks on the Mountain in 1934, no less than three hundred
were returned emigrants from the United States, and quotes as a significant
example the case of Father Galaktyon, the guest-master at Koutloumousiou,
who during fifteen years in the New World had opened a total of fifty-five
cafés and restaurants, each of which he had shortly afterwards had to close
"because the creditors insisted".[21] Not all these men are despairing; some are

22
Eighteenth-century frescoes
in the seldom-used refectory
at Vatopedi, an idior-
rhythmic monastery where
monks usually eat separately

[21] CHOUKAS, op. cit.

simply lazy, and there are always those, widowers perhaps, who have no one left to live for and so devote their savings to the purchase of a serene and secure, if not actually a comfortable, old age. To them must be added the political refugees – especially in the non-Greek monasteries – and, finally, the out-and-out criminals, sure of a permanent asylum, whose numbers just before the last war were estimated at between fifty and sixty.

For all this second category there will be moments of anguish as they try to readjust body, mind and spirit to the requirements of monastic life. A few may accomplish the gear-change smoothly enough, but most will discover that it takes more than an adopted name and an enforced residence on the Mountain to sever all emotional links with the outside world. One of my own most improbable Athonite experiences occurred during my first visit, in the monastery of Simopetra, when I was roused late at night by an aged monk who led me on tiptoe to his cell and there, in conditions of almost melodramatic secrecy (since all musical instruments are forbidden) bade me explain to him the workings of his portable tape-recorder. I did so as best I could; but when he then extracted a transistor radio from inside his mattress and asked how to link the two devices together so that he could record those of his favourite programmes that were broadcast during the hours he was in church, I had to admit defeat. He was a touching figure, childlike in his pride in the new toys he had so mysteriously acquired as well as in the pleasure he obviously took in hiding them from his superiors. But he was not *megaloskhimos* material. I could not help feeling, as I groped my way back to bed, that he should never have come to Athos in the first place; he probably suspected as much himself.

But however great the differences between those for whom the Holy Mountain represents the only way and those for whom it is merely the easy way, there is one characteristic that virtually all Athonite monks seem to share – a deep and utterly unquestioning faith not only in the existence but in the immediate presence of God, tempered always by the equally certain knowledge that the Devil also is not far off. Nothing occurs except by the will of one or the other, and thus a cogent and wholly satisfactory explanation is ready to hand for every eventuality. Consider, for example, the following pronouncement, made by one of the elders of Esphigmenou to Dr Choukas in 1934, on the subject of the newly installed telephone:

> "The explanation for its working is very simple. Satan stations inferior devils at the ends, and they carry the words to the ears of the listeners. I can stop that satanic device from functioning by just touching it with this holy cross and mentioning the name of the Virgin."

Father Spyridon of the Lavra, a former medical officer in the Greek Army who wrote an extremely learned book on his monastery in 1930, was prepared to go even further. Deeply shocked by the marriage in 1921 of the Greek Crown Prince (later George II) to a Roumanian princess while his sister married her brother – a combination falling well within the proscribed degrees of affinity – and refusing to accept the argument that since the two marriages were simultaneous neither could invalidate the other, he had no hesitation in attributing to this incestuous arrangement the later misfortunes of both royal houses and the subsequent expulsion of the Greek populations of Asia Minor.

Such opinions are harmless enough; but they are, alas, manifestations of a more serious ill. That spirit of uncompromising reaction that never forgave the efforts of various Byzantine Emperors to reunite the Eastern and Western Churches has lost none of its force with the passage of time; preserved and nourished throughout the years of Turkish domination, protected alike from outside influence and from new ideas, it has finally emerged in the twentieth century as a blind and monumental bigotry that both infuriates and stultifies. Just as the monks are reminded daily by the beat of the semandron that the Orthodox Church is the Ark of Salvation, so are most of them equally persuaded that all those of other faiths, those who maintain that the Holy Ghost proceeds from the Son as well as from the Father or those who cross themselves with four fingers from left to right, are irretrievably damned. As is perhaps to be expected after the Fourth Crusade, it is the Roman Catholics for whom they feel the greatest antipathy; that pillar of highest Victorian Anglicanism, Mr

Athelstan Riley, records the following conversation with one of the elders of
Stavronikita in 1883:

> "Of course," said the epitropos . . . "of course it is a well-known fact that
> all Roman priests are immoral."
>
> "No," I replied; "that is not true. You have never been in Roman
> Catholic countries whilst this English priest and I have seen much of the
> Roman clergy, and we know that there are as good men amongst them as
> anywhere in Christendom."
>
> "Well, the greater number are immoral," urged the epitropos.
>
> "Few of them," said I.
>
> "A great many," said the epitropos.
>
> "Very few," said I.[22]

For a Catholic, therefore, who desires the most favourable treatment from a
monastery and does not fall into the special category of Distinguished Visitor,
only one course can be unreservedly recommended in the face of the inevitable
question as to his religion – that of temporary apostasy. Anglican readers, on
the other hand, will be gratified to learn that they can normally expect pity
rather than hostility; such suspicions as they may from time to time incur will,
more often than not, be dispelled by the words "But my Church is in communion with yours", reverently – if a little reproachfully – intoned with the
hands loosely clasped in front of the body. (To clasp them behind the back is
considered in the highest degree disrespectful.) In the atmosphere prevailing on
the Mountain today, however, it is difficult to imagine any repetition of those
occasions when Riley's companion, the Reverend A. B. Owen, was actually
permitted to celebrate the Anglican liturgy at both Vatopedi and the Lavra – in
the presence, let it be noted, of so distinguished a divine as the Archbishop of
Kavalla, who later informed the monkish congregation that the incomprehensible words to which they had been listening were in fact an original composition by St Gregory the Great.

Where bigotry leads, prudery is quick to follow. Some monasteries tend to

[22] A. RILEY, *Athos, or the Mountain of the Monks*, London, 1887.

23
A konak (or "embassy") of
one of the Ruling Monasteries
to the central government
at Karyes

be more broadminded than others, but in all of them it is as well to be on one's guard lest monkish susceptibilities be offended. Washing, for example, is always a problem. "He who is once washed in Christ," wrote St Jerome, "needs not to wash again." This fearful dictum accurately summarizes the general monastic attitude to soap and water. They are not considered sinful, merely unnecessary; and though one or two monasteries have installed guest bathrooms of a kind, in most houses the visitors' efforts in the cause of hygiene are regarded with an amused and faintly patronising forbearance as he crouches with sponge and toothbrush beneath the single spluttering tap at the foot of the main staircase. The same is true of his laundry. On Athos, where mules are nowadays less plentiful than they were, it is unwise to travel with more clothes or equipment than can conveniently be carried on the back; and, as the sun is hot and the paths dusty, a few minutes each day at the wash-tub are rarely ill-spent. Seldom on the Mountain have I ever seen monks' garments hanging out to dry; but nevertheless most monasteries provide some rudimentary clothes-line to accommodate the whims of the passing traveller.

The Grand Lavra possesses both a clothes-line and a wash-house. Being also the largest and among the most frequently visited of Athonite foundations, it might have been supposed to be relatively enlightened in these matters. Alas, it is not – as I learnt within a few hours of my arrival. My first shock came when I was requested, politely but firmly, by the guest-master to remove a pair of under-pants then fluttering happily from the line. This, he pointed out, was a mon-astery; shirts, socks, handkerchiefs, even vests, might be dried with propriety within its walls. But underpants were a shameful abomination and could on no account be permitted. Meekly, I obeyed; but worse was to come. I woke the following morning at dawn. The monks were, as usual, in church; my fellow-guests were still asleep; the whole monastery lay in silence. I had un-fortunately ignored the advice of Athelstan Riley, who recommends all travellers to Athos to provide themselves with a "portable india-rubber bath", but this seemed the perfect opportunity to do the best I could without one; and I made quietly for the wash-house. Its principal furnishing was a huge stone trough; and into this I now clambered, turning on all four of the taps set at regular intervals along its length and covering myself from head to foot in a deep and

24
Headquarters of the mon-astic government of Athos with the church of the Protaton and its bell-tower in the foreground

D

luxurious lather. At this point the guest-master appeared. He was a youngish man and, clearly, a fanatic; he took one look at me and exploded. Never have I seen anyone so angry. The flood of hysterical Greek that poured from the depths of that enormous beard was largely incomprehensible to me, but his message was plain. For the second time in twelve hours I had desecrated his monastery. Having already offended God and the Mother of God with the spectacle of my underpants I was now compounding the sacrilege by standing stark naked under the very roof of the Grand Lavra. I was the Whore of Babylon, I was Sodom and Gomorrah, I was a minion of Satan sent to corrupt the Holy Mountain. I was to put on my scabrous clothes at once and return with all speed to the foul pit whence I had come.

This time I felt genuinely aggrieved. There were several questions I should have liked to ask. How could one wash properly with one's clothes on? Might one never wash the lower half of the body at all? Did monks never do so? Come to that, did they ever wash the upper half? Was nudity never permitted? Was it a sin? If one could not strip when alone in a wash-room, where could one strip? And whom was I shocking? God? But had not God designed me in the first place? Him, the guest-master? Then why didn't he go away? And incidentally, why wasn't he in Church where he belonged?

But language failed, and without language how can resolution remain firm? Hastily pulling trousers back over still-soapy legs, I retreated to the dormitory, wondering only how this outraged vigilante would have reacted to the vision of Mr Athelstan Riley in all that india-rubber.

In retrospect, the incident was laughable enough; yet it is a perfect indication of what can happen when sexual repression reaches the point of ultimate absurdity. Nowhere in the world outside Athos is even the sight of a woman unknown, even the thought of one – the *Panaghia* alone excepted – sinful. In these circumstances sex can no longer be despised or belittled – though that would be unpleasant enough – but becomes instead something to be feared, which is infinitely worse. And so hugely does this fear loom in many an Athonite mind that the merest suggestion of its existence is fraught with peril. Such suggestions must therefore be avoided at all costs; and a hysterical, unreasoning prudery is the inevitable result.

But prudery is not necessarily the child of fear; it can also be born of guilt, which it may seek either to atone for or to conceal. For countless generations of Greeks, the sexual habits of Athonite monks have provided an unfailing source of ribald anecdote and lubricious speculation. How much homosexuality, in fact, exists on Athos it is clearly impossible to say. Certainly some – as in any community from which, for whatever reason it may be, one sex or the other is altogether excluded. In the idiorrhythmic monasteries especially, where opportunities are greater and where it is still the custom for a young novice to be attached to an older monk and to live with him in the joint capacity of servant and disciple, some suspicions are unavoidable. It should also be remembered that the existence of homosexuality has always been accepted in the Near East, where, thanks to Hellenistic broadmindedness and sense of proportion, public opinion has never failed – as so lamentably in the West – to see it in its proper perspective. On the other hand, the general atmosphere in the monasteries, as it strikes the normal visitor, is not such as to suggest an unbridled licentiousness. For a monk as for any other human being, lifelong chastity is hard; but for nearly all of them the disciplines of Athos have been freely chosen, and all must understand – or if they do not, they must soon learn – that that peace of mind which is the greatest gift that the Mountain has to offer can only be won on the Mountain's own terms.

*　　*　　*

In the second half of the nineteenth century two main features characterized the Eastern European political scene – the steady decadence of the Ottoman Empire and the proportionately increasing determination on the part of Russia to gain control of the Black Sea Straits. The Sick Man of Europe was entering his last decline. That great upsurge of nationalist consciousness sparked by the French Revolution had already sapped much of his strength; Serbia and Greece had been the first to wrench themselves free, and their efforts had set off a chain reaction of revolutionary fervour which was to inflame the entire Balkan peninsula for the rest of the century. Meanwhile, Ottoman military power failed utterly to recover from the loss of the Janissaries, executed *en masse* – they numbered some twenty-five thousand – by a panicky Mahmud II in 1826; the Civil Service, once the wonder and admiration of Europe, sank ever deeper into a stew of apathy and corruption; and, in the fetid atmosphere of Constantinople, one Sultan after another cringed among his eunuchs and his concubines, worn out by sexual excesses and half crazed by alcohol and aphrodisiacs, while his Empire crumbled into ruin around him.

As Turkey weakened, Russia grew stronger; and as she grew stronger, her need for a free outlet to the Mediterranean, on which she depended for almost half of her seaborne export trade, became ever more urgent. The first step towards this goal was to increase her influence, at Ottoman expense, in south-east Europe; and so there began, around the middle of the century, a great new Russian diplomatic offensive throughout the Balkans. Nowhere, acre for acre, were her attentions more assiduously pressed than on the Holy Mountain.

There was nothing new in the idea of a Russian monastery on Mount Athos. One had already existed in the twelfth century, and several of the Ruling Monasteries had at various periods in the past been dominated by Slavs – though usually Serbs or Bulgars – until sooner or later they had fallen on evil days and were bought up and re-endowed by wealthy Greeks. That of St Pantaleimon had an old Russian tradition, but it was a purely Greek house when, in 1834, fifteen young Russian monks appeared. They were joined by a further contingent; then by another, and another, until the Russians at last outnumbered the Greeks and began pressing for special rights – first, to hold services in their own language on alternate days, and then, a few years later, to elect a Russian abbot. By now the Athonite authorities were growing uneasy, and this last request they categorically refused; but in 1875 the Oecumenical Patriarch, persuaded by the irresistible generosity of the Russian Ambassador to the Sublime Porte, overruled them. The remaining Greeks were ousted, and the way seemed clear for renewed expansion.

The Holy Synod was quite right to be alarmed, well knowing that this steady infiltration had no connection with any religious or monastic revival in Russia itself; it was the beginning of a deliberate and utterly cold-blooded attempt to take over the whole of Athos, to swamp it by sheer weight of numbers. Once the Mountain was in Russian hands it could be used as a sort of Balkan Gibraltar, a virtually impregnable base from which to dominate the north-eastern Mediter-

25
Street scene in Karyes

ranean. More important still, there could be no better way of breaking the power of the Greek Church, a vital preliminary to Russia's ultimate objective – the expulsion of Turkey from Eastern Europe, the absolute control of the Bosphorus and the Dardanelles and, finally, the long-delayed assumption by the Tsar of his rightful heritage, the Throne of the Emperors at Constantinople.

With the outbreak of war between the two Empires in 1877, it looked as though these dreams would soon be realised. The Russian Army was already at San Stefano – only seven miles from the Turkish capital – when, early the following year, the Sultan was forced to sue for peace terms. Constantinople was left for the time being, but the last vestiges of Ottoman control were to be removed from Serbia, Montenegro, Roumania and Bosnia-Herzegovina, while a new "Greater Bulgaria", to be formed under Russian suzerainty, was to include the bulk of Macedonia and Thrace – including, of course, the Holy Mountain. Finally, lest there should be any remaining doubts as to their intentions where Athos was concerned, a special clause was inserted by which the Russian monks were guaranteed equal rights with those of all other nationalities.

They were harsh conditions, and if the Treaty of San Stefano had ever come into force, the last hundred years of Athonite and indeed Eastern European history would have been very different; but the Russians had miscalculated. They had reckoned on the benevolent non-intervention of the Western Powers.

> We don't want to fight, but by jingo if we do,
> We've got the men, we've got the ships, we've got the money too;
> We've fought the Bear before, and while Britons shall be true,
> The Russians shall not have Constantinople!

Thus sang the English music-halls of 1878, although strictly speaking the Russians had not yet asked for it. Austria and Prussia felt much the same way; and so it was that, when Russia was forced to submit the Treaty of San Stefano for ratification by the Congress of Berlin three months later, most of its terms were rejected out of hand. Thanks largely to Disraeli, some two-thirds of the territory ceded by Turkey at San Stefano was returned to her; and Mount Athos remained, after all, under the suzerainty of the Ottoman Empire. But the Treaty of Berlin, by which the Congress set a seal on its new dispensations,

26
The church at Koutlou-
mousiou, a cenobitic
monastery on the outskirts
of Karyes

retained with only a slight change of emphasis the specific provision relating
to the Holy Mountain on which the Russians had insisted at San Stefano. Article
62 of the final draft ran as follows: "The monks of Mount Athos, whatever their
country of origin, shall be maintained in their former possessions and advantages
and shall enjoy, without any exception, complete equality of rights and
privileges."

It was a curious formula in which to enshrine the first international recognition,
after more than nine centuries, of the special status of the Mountain; but it gave
the Russians all the encouragement they needed to go ahead with their previous
policy. They now set to work in earnest. Their attempts to gain control of
Iveron (with Georgian monks, according to the monastery's ancient tradition),   ILL. 29
Koutloumousiou and the arsenal of Stavronikita – all, significantly, on or near   ILL. 26
the east coast of the peninsula, had failed; but they had no difficulty in buying
the leases of the two sketes of St Elias and St Andrew, together with some
twenty kellia. All their possessions, including their Ruling Monastery of St
Pantaleimon, were hugely and hideously enlarged; St Pantaleimon – or, as it is
more generally known, Russico – looks from the sea more like a barracks than a
monastery, and the two sketes (aesthetically very little better) were crammed
with new recruits until each equalled or exceeded it in population. The next
stage was to obtain for these sketes the status of Ruling Monasteries, thereby
giving them a representative – and a vote – at Karyes; and a formal request in
this sense was accordingly made to Constantinople. Fortunately for Athos, the
new Patriarch was immune to the usual sweeteners and put his foot down. The
Ruling Monasteries were fixed at twenty; no increases to their number could
in any circumstances be permitted. But still the steady immigration continued,
until by 1903 the Slavs, with a total monkish population of well over four thousand, found themselves in a majority on the Mountain. Already twenty years
before, Athelstan Riley had written: "It cannot be disguised that Russico has
more concern with politics than religion"; by now his words had not only
proved true – they were seen to be an understatement.

If this tide had continued to flow unchecked, it is unlikely that the authorities
at Karyes or Constantinople would have been able to resist it for very much
longer. But now for the second time in forty years the monks were saved from

the prospect of Russian domination – this time for ever, and by the one event for which they and all their spiritual forefathers had been waiting for nearly five centuries. In the autumn of 1912, during the first Balkan War, King Constantine of Greece captured Salonica; and on November 2 of that same year the Holy Mountain was at last delivered from the shadow of Islam. The four Powers who were subsequently appointed to share with Russia the responsibility of deciding on its future proved unsympathetic to all suggestions for a further increase in Slavonic influence, and the tortuous diplomacy of St Petersburg found itself powerless.

Once more, and once more only, was the Russian temperament seriously to disturb the peace of Athos. This was when a monk at the skete of St Andrew, a former hussar by the name of Anthony Bulatovitch, was vouchsafed a revelation to the effect that the Name of God, being an integral part of God, was itself divine. When this theory failed to recommend itself to his superiors, the whole Russian community on the Mountain was rent from top to bottom; and the events that followed, during which the heretical monks starved out and finally evicted those of more orthodox persuasion, were brought to a head by the arrival, on June 24, 1913, of a Russian warship carrying on board an Archbishop and – lest even his authority should prove insufficient – a sizeable detachment of troops. Three weeks later the differences were finally settled by the storming of St Pantaleimon by the troops and a subsequent pitched battle between them and the heretics, who had by this time taken to the woods. As a result no less than six hundred and sixteen monks were deported – mostly to Siberia – and, as the Holy Synod at Moscow later somewhat unexpectedly admitted, "the forty with criminal records were imprisoned at Odessa". After this incident the Russian chances of Athonite domination looked slim indeed; but before long the repercussions of a Sarajevo pistol-shot had forced upon the conference-tables of Europe other more urgent preoccupations.

*   *   *

The story of the "liberation" of Mount Athos from the Turks has come down to us in a vivid account by a French eye-witness who chanced to find himself at the Lavra on the very day that the Greek fleet of Condouriotis appeared over the horizon. His tale of breathless monks swarming on to the monastery battlements, of centuries-old cannon bursting out their *feu-de-joie*, of Greek flags being run up over the length and breadth of a mountain loud with the unaccustomed pealing of bells, makes thrilling reading even today; but the page that lingers most persistently in the memory is that which records his conversation with the Turkish *kaimakam*, sitting philosophically on his divan in Karyes while he awaits his inevitable arrest.

"Look around you," says the kaimakam. "Look at these thousands of monks; visit their monasteries, question them yourself. Of what, in reality, can they complain? Have we touched their rules? Have we violated their property? Have we forbidden their pilgrimages? Have we altered even a tittle of their secular constitution? . . . What race, I ask you, what conqueror could have treated these people with greater humanity, greater moderation, greater religious tolerance? Under our law they have remained no less free, indeed freer, than under the Byzantine Emperors. . . . And they have not had to endure under our domination a hundredth part of the vexations that you have imposed on your monks in France. . . . *Allez, Monsieur!* They will regret us. Greeks, Russians, Serbs, Roumanians, Bulgars, all those monks hate each other like poison. They are bound together only by their common loathing of Islam. When we are no longer there, they will tear each other to pieces. . . ."[23]

But for the First World War, these gloomy prognostications might well have proved justified; but when, a decade later, the smoke at last cleared from the eastern Mediterranean, the Holy Mountain was seen to be fully and firmly established under Greek protection, in conditions which guaranteed the continuation of all its traditional rights and liberties. These conditions, first stipulated in the Treaty of Sèvres in 1920 and ratified three years later at Lausanne, were further elaborated by the Athonite community itself and in 1924 submitted to the Greek Government through – the point should be noted – its Ministry of Foreign Affairs; and they are now embodied in the Hellenic constitution. By its terms, every monk of Athos, whatever his country of origin, is deemed to be a Greek subject. He is liable neither to military service nor to

[23] JEROME and JEAN THARAUD, *La Bataille à Scutari*. Quoted by ROBERT BYRON, *The Station*, London, 1928.

27
Churches in the Russian skete of St Andrew's outside Karyes

28 (overleaf)
On the landing-stage at Xenophontos

normal taxation. Freedom from customs duties extends to all monastic exports and the large majority of imports. Justice – except in penal cases, which are referred to the ordinary courts in Salonica – is entrusted to the Holy Synod at Karyes, as is the complete administration of the domestic affairs of the Mountain. The Greek Governor, sitting alone and celibate at what must be his service's most unpopular post, is virtually powerless; he is bound to uphold any constitutional decision of the Synod and thus serves as little more than a mouthpiece for his Government, to which he is responsible, as always, through the Foreign Ministry.

The Holy Synod itself is composed of twenty monks, one from each of the Ruling Monasteries. They are appointed for a year, during which time they reside – at least in theory – at Karyes and make up the parliament of the Holy Mountain. Executive power, however, is vested in the *Epistasia*, a smaller body of four members of the Synod, drawn according to a system which ensures the regular representation of each monastery in turn; and the president of this, chosen by monastic seniority, is known as the *Protepistates*, the Premier monk of Athos. He and his three colleagues each hold one quarter of the Great Seal of the community; thus they have little power as individuals, but when acting together they are supreme. They it is who take the day-to-day decisions of Athonite government; they who are responsible for the cleanliness and public services, such as they are, of Karyes; they, finally, who administer the Athonite police force. These awesome veterans have now alas been shorn of the voluminous white shirts, pompommed clogs and yellow velvet breeches which accounted for much of their pre-war splendour; but their beards and staffs of office, and the proud two-headed eagles of Byzantium on their caps remain as imposing as ever, while they enforce the age-old regulations against drunkenness and secular song, and otherwise maintain that decorum properly befitting the capital of what is, with the Vatican City, the last remaining theocracy in the world.

Yet the authority of the Epistasia, extensive as it is in all matters relating to the Mountain as a whole, counts for little enough in the individual monasteries. Here any outside interference is bitterly resented – especially if it comes from the Greek Government in Athens. When possible the daily routine of Greek-Athonite relations is handled by the Governor at Karyes through the Epistasia;

but when from time to time it becomes necessary to make a direct approach to one monastery or another, the sparks are apt to fly – particularly if the point at issue touches, as it usually does, on the delicate question of culture.

The monks of Athos still cherish unresolved feelings about the works of art of which they are guardians. On the one hand, they are justifiably proud that their monasteries should harbour objects of such value and venerable antiquity (though a large number are not quite so old as they imagine) as to bring connoisseurs and scholars from all over the world to examine them. On the other, they remain jealous and possessive, ashamed of the depredations suffered during the past hundred and fifty years alone, when unscrupulous visitors – like the Hon. Robert Curzon in 1837 – took advantage of the innocence and gullibility of their predecessors and stripped the Mountain of many of its more easily removable treasures; and they are, above all, determined that such occurrences shall not be repeated. This makes them particularly sensitive to suggestions of the kind sometimes made in the Greek press to the effect that the principal works of art remaining on Mount Athos should be transferred to Athenian museums and libraries, with the unmistakable inference that they are unable to look after their own property. It also breeds an intense suspicion of the government inspectors who occasionally tour the Mountain to examine, catalogue or restore, and of the frequent requests from cultural bodies to loan their treasures for temporary exhibitions. (The comprehensive UNESCO exhibition of Byzantine Art held in Athens in 1964 contained, among well over a thousand items, only one from Athos – a late fourteenth-century icon from the monastery of the Pantocrator.)

The *bona fide* visitor, genuinely anxious to see the best that a given monastery has to offer, will probably find the monks co-operative enough; but even he should not necessarily expect the way to be smooth before him. Sooner or later he, too, will be told that the key to the treasury is lost, or that Father Theophylact who keeps it has regrettably left for Karyes, or that only the Abbot has the power to grant his requests and that the Abbot can on no account be disturbed. On such occasions he will need patience, tact and – most important of all, if he does not himself speak Greek – a first-rate interpreter. If, with these, he is able to persuade the monastic authorities that he is not just another of those Central European hitch-hikers with whom the Mountain has in recent years been plagued, who look to it simply for a free holiday and have neither knowledge of nor interest in anything for which it stands, then they may conceivably change their attitude; but he must also face the occasional possibility of being sent – intellectually speaking – empty away.

Such a fate may be humiliating, but it is not in most cases calamitous. For the truth is that the treasures of Athos, though nearly always interesting and often beautiful, are rarely in themselves sublime. One or two, admittedly, catch at the breath; the Nicephorus Phocas Bible, for example, or the two small mosaics in the new church of Xenophontos, or the so-called "St Pulcheria's cup", an exquisite paten of carved ophite preserved at Xeropotamou. Several others fascinate for their associations, like the monumentally hideous jasper receptacle presented to Vatopedi by Manuel Cantacuzene, son of John VI, with its dire warnings of what, five hundred years later, was to be described as *art nouveau* by a deluded posterity. For the rest, there is little to compare with the beauties that may be found at the Victoria and Albert or the Vatican, Dumbarton Oaks or the Bibliothèque Nationale, let alone that most magical to me of all Byzantine treasure-houses, the Benaki Museum in Athens.

Where relics are concerned, the situation is very different. In this unsavoury field, Mount Athos must stand supreme among all the shrines of Orthodox Christendom. Now, at last, the monks feel themselves on home ground, and their entire attitude reflects their confidence. In the Athonite view, works of secular beauty or learning do not elevate the soul to God and are, arguably, even sinful; but a holy relic is an intercession. It demands and deserves constant veneration, and must in consequence be exhibited and adored as frequently as possible. Never, therefore, will the visitor – provided only that he maintains a properly respectful attitude – encounter any reluctance on the part of the monks to display their grisly souvenirs. Day after day, in one monastery after another, he ILLS 36 & 41 will find himself waiting inside the church while the priest, having robed himself suitably for the occasion, lays out the cream of the monastic collection on a long trestle table; he will then attend, looking as credulous as he can, while the nature of the exhibits and their miraculous properties if any are carefully explained to him; finally, when these preliminaries are completed, he will move slowly along the line in the manner of royalty inspecting a cup final team – except that, unlike royalty, he will be expected to kiss each item as he passes.

A few, but only a few, of these items are memorable; pieces of wood from the True Cross, for example, of which Athos possesses more than any other community – most of it, in magnificent reliquaries, at Xeropotamou and the Lavra; or, perhaps, the Virgin's girdle at Vatopedi which was lent to Constantinople in 1872, at the request of the Sultan, in order to check an epidemic of cholera. Otherwise, all accurate recollection becomes lost in a great splintery stew of skulls and jawbones, of fingers and feet and fibias, and endless successions of desiccated teeth. There is no escape from these depressing arrays – of whose genuineness, it is hardly necessary to add, no monk entertains a moment's doubt; one can only hope for the occasional unexpected consolation furnished by such objects as the tusk of St Christopher, now reverently preserved at Dionysiou. This saint, unrelated to the overworked preserver of the western motorist, was born – for reasons not altogether clear – with the head of a dog; on his conversion to Christianity, however, his countenance assumed a human shape of such outstanding beauty that he was able himself effortlessly to convert no less than forty-eight thousand persons, including the courtesans sent to seduce him.[24] Among the frescoes of Athonite churches he is a familiar figure, being invariably portrayed in his pre-conversion form – a tradition which must not only have made things a lot easier for the artist but also allows the beholder the joy of instant recognition.

Half-way between the true works of art and the relics come the miraculous icons. They cannot, in all honesty, be included in the former category, first, because nearly all the best icons on the Mountain were removed by an unscupulous Russian called Uspensky (who did even more damage in the pictorial field than Curzon in the literary), and secondly because the effective visibility of a popular icon seems to vary in inverse ratio to its wonder-working properties. Athos possesses several which are very miraculous indeed. Nearly all, inevitably,

[24] Such at least is the version preferred by Robert Byron. An alternative story is that St Christopher's natural beauty made him so irresistible that, to avoid the dangers of sin, he prayed for uglification. His story then bears comparison with that of St Wilgeforte, magnificently commemorated in the Church of St Etienne at Beauvais, who in answer to a similar prayer found herself covered by a thick black bushy beard to the ankles.

30
The church at Philotheou

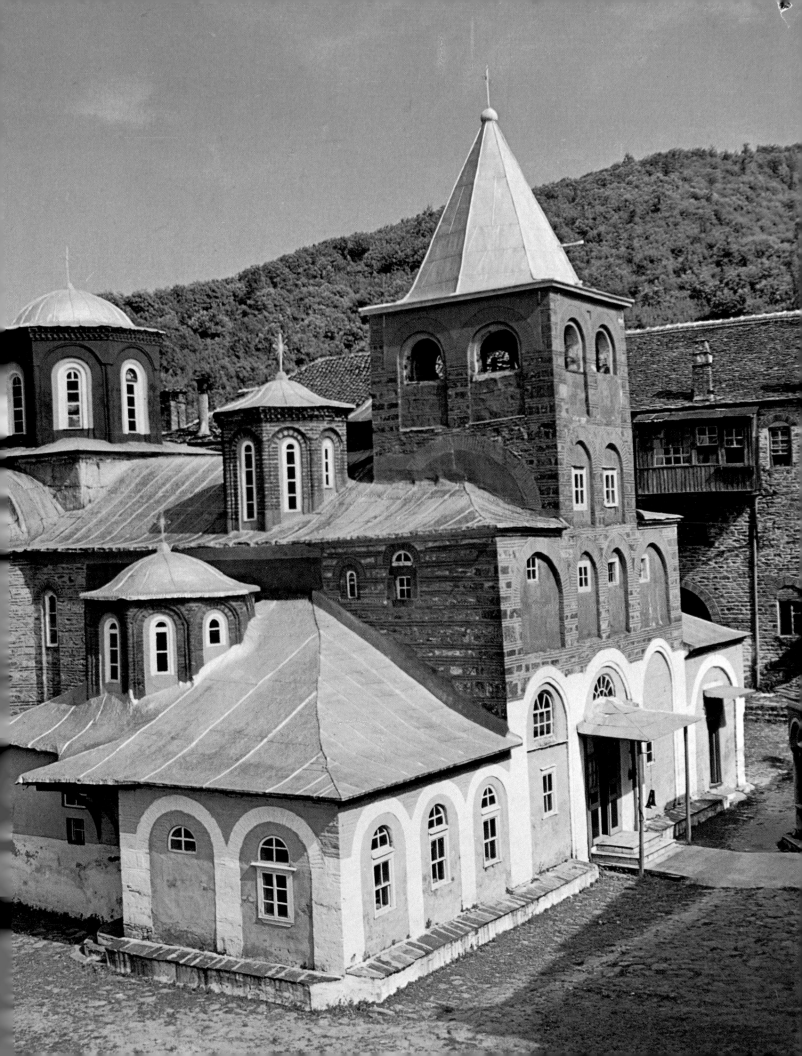

are of the Virgin. There she is, as the Trikheiroussa of Chilandar, her third hand stuck on in the eighth century by St John Damascene after his own hand, amputated by the Caliph, had been restored by her intercession; or as the Portaïtissa of Iveron who, having floated upright over the sea from Nicaea to escape the iconoclast persecutions, refused to remain in the church but returned time after time to the same place by the main gate, where she now occupies a special chapel. (The Trikheiroussa is almost certainly a fourteenth-century work, and in iconoclast times Iveron had not yet been built; but details of this nature are of little interest to the Athonite mind, and to insist on them is not only bad manners – it is to miss the point.) There she is again, the gentle Glykophiloussa of Philotheou, one of those innumerable portraits done from the life by that prolific if somewhat limited painter St Luke, of which the Holy Mountain properly possesses its full share. All these icons have one thing in common. Encrusted with that hideous *orfèvrerie* with which the Orthodox faithful love to adorn the objects of their veneration, hung round with votive offerings – coins, jewels, sometimes even wrist-watches – and blackened by the smoky adoration of the centuries, they are all, as near as makes no difference, invisible. And therein, perhaps, lies their mystery.

ILLS 15, 16, 21, 46 & 50

And so we are left with the frescoes. Like nearly all western Europeans of his time, the Hon. Robert Curzon was frankly unappreciative. The churches of Athos, he wrote, contain "only coarse paintings in fresco representing saints in the conventional Greek style of superlative ugliness. . . . It is difficult to conceive how anyone, even in the dark ages, can have been simple enough to look upon these quaint and absurd paintings with feelings of religious awe; but some of the monks of the Holy Mountain do so even now." The Elgin of the Athonite libraries had every right to his opinions on church decoration; but, to the modern eye at least, it is here that the artistic traditions of the Holy Mountain appear at their most striking and most successful. However divided their predecessors may have been on the question a century ago, the modern inhabitants of Athos seem to share this view. They are usually only too happy to show off the beauties of their katholikons and refectories. In doing so, they may often reveal a marked ignorance of history and even, on occasion, a surprising sketchiness of scriptural

31
Father Photios, guardian of the chapel of the Prodromos at Karyes

32
Reliquaries at Vatopedi

knowledge; their taste, likewise, is seldom impeccable. But awe they have in plenty; and they are not alone.

In these frescoes it is not the individual artistry of one painting or another that impresses, though much of the work radiates imagination and vitality. It is, rather, the cumulative impact of hundreds of square feet of wall and dome, of embrasure and pendentive, each painstakingly designed to form an integral part of the overall scheme and worked upon until, in accordance with the strictest canons of Byzantine iconography, not a cranny remains that does not tell its own chapter of the Christian story. The biblical scenes, preconceived from nursery days, now take on a new complexion as one sees them, each in its appointed place, endlessly repeated in church after church across the Mountain; the fixed solemnity of the infant Christ, already prefiguring from the manger that glowering gaze with which, as the great All-Ruler, he transfixes the world from the heights of the topmost dome; the Virgin, smiling in gentle contrast at her new-born son – for in the Orthodox world she is the ever-merciful, he the stern and unforgiving – or, over the west door, lying in the marble majesty of her dormition, while the crouching disciples form sorrowful parabolas round her bed. The four-square directness of the Baptism, where the regular ripples of Jordan conveniently solve the problem of the Saviour's nudity; Adam and Eve, their stomachs pointedly bereft of navels; the voracious monsters of Hell, the tormented tombstones of Purgatory, all become gratifyingly familiar. So, even, do the rows of portraits. And thus the early fathers of the Church, the archangels and saints, the patriarchs and the emperors, John the Baptist in his skins, St Simeon on his pillar, inescapably remind an ex-diplomat of the local characters and officials of some foreign capital to which he has been newly posted; at first nameless and faceless nonentities, after a week of official receptions they begin to assume characters of their own, and almost imperceptibly become part of the life around him.

*   *   *

In this essay I have tried to interweave the history of the Holy Mountain with the life of the monks who inhabit it today and the impressions that it makes on the twentieth-century visitor; and if I have been tempted to shuttle too frequently up and down the centuries I can only plead that in a community which has probably shown less change in the last thousand years than anywhere else in the civilised world, the concepts of past and present have little meaning. More important – and disturbing – to the monks of Athos is the future. This they can never afford to ignore; for however hard they may try to isolate themselves from the outside world they know it is on this, ultimately, that their future depends.

Athos has seen the deaths of many men, but the birth of none. Thus, if life is to continue on the Mountain, it can only do so by the constant transfusion of new blood from beyond its borders. In the past, even during the centuries of Turkish rule, this new blood has always been forthcoming. Now it seems that the source is drying up. What used to be a steady flow has become the meagrest of trickles. The figures speak for themselves. In 1903 the total monkish population was 7,432. In 1928 it had decreased to 4,858. The last count, of 1959, yielded a figure of 1,641. In other words, the Athonite community is diminishing at a present rate of about one hundred every year. This, if it were to continue, would mean the end of Athos as we know it by about 1975; but such a calculation ignores the fact that most of the monks are already old men, and as the average age rises, so the death rate will increase. Later it will probably fall again, since such young monks as have come to the Mountain in the past decade or so may be expected to live more than another ten years; but these alone will be powerless to prevent the decline. Athonite monasteries are designed to accommodate several hundred monks each; many are crumbling through lack of maintenance, and they cannot be kept going by a mere handful of ageing men.

Desperate as the situation is, it is all too easy to explain. During the first years of this century the monasteries of Athos, most of whose large and profitable estates on the mainland, in Greece and elsewhere, had not yet been confiscated by grasping governments,[25] were still for the most part rich and prosperous. A poor young peasant, by becoming a monk, would be assured of a standard of living certainly not lower and probably a good deal higher than he might reasonably have expected in his village. In the inter-war years, with the gradual development of the Greek economy and the seizure by the Greek Government

[25] The new Roumanian state, in an anti-Hellenist outburst, did in fact confiscate Athonite property in 1863, and the Russians rather half-heartedly followed suit ten years later. But much of the property was later recovered.

in 1925, for a quite unrealistic rental, of all the mainland estates of the monasteries for the resettlement of the refugees from Asia Minor, the incentives were less; but they still held good to some extent, and any family that could boast an Athonite monk within its circle would find its social status considerably enhanced. But in the last ten years the situation has changed. The country is richer, the monasteries poorer and generally considered to be moribund. Affluence has encouraged materialism; and the Church, having long since forfeited its position as defender-in-chief of Hellenistic ideals, is now losing much of its remaining religious prestige. The monks who not long ago were revered for their wisdom and saintliness, as well as for the beauty of their way of life, are now more often ridiculed, however unjustly, by their countrymen as a bunch of foolish old perverts who have failed to keep up with the times.

Such an analysis could be developed almost indefinitely; but it would be a pointless exercise. The fundamental, unanswerable fact is that Mount Athos has become an anachronism, and one which modern Greece is no longer able to indulge. Ironically enough, it is in the communist countries of Eastern Europe that the call of the Holy Mountain seems most clearly heard. In 1964 the Soviet Government agreed to release a few Russian novices – the first since the Revolution – to St Pantaleimon, and Marshal Tito has done the same for Chilandar – following this gesture, according to a recent report, with the gift of an electric generator. But such recruits, welcome as they may be, cannot hope to buttress the whole community against the onslaught of a hostile age. Unless a miracle happens – a great nation-wide religious revival, nothing less – the Holy Mountain is doomed. The smaller monasteries will presumably go first, sending such senile survivors as are no longer able to look after themselves to their more populous neighbours – the Lavra, perhaps, or Vatopedi – where they can be cared for till they die. These two monasteries, and conceivably a few others, may limp on a little longer; they might even manage to continue indefinitely. But Mount Athos as we know it will be gone.

What, then, will be its future? No one can tell. Already in the nineteen-twenties, during the mercifully short-lived régime of General Pangalos, it was suggested that all the monasteries should be disbanded and a gigantic holiday resort, complete with dance-halls and casino, erected in their place. The idea was

33
The Madonna "Axión estin" ("Worthy it is"), the holiest icon on Athos, preserved in the church of the Protaton at Karyes

then ruled out by the terms of the Athonite Constitution; but when there is no longer a Holy Synod to invoke this Constitution, some similar scheme may be put forward. This time, if tourist-worship continues at its present pitch of intensity, opposition will be harder. Fortunately there are other less ghastly possibilities. If ever Greek–Turkish relations deteriorate, because of Cyprus or for any other reason, to the point where the Oecumenical Patriarch is forced to leave Istanbul, he will most probably instal himself on Athos – unless, that is, the casino has got there first – and so save the situation for a little while longer. From the Athonite point of view, this would clearly be the best solution of all; but even the Patriarch would be hard put to it to save the whole Mountain from secular hands. Yet another hope might be for all or part of the peninsula to be taken over by some great learned or charitable foundation – Dumbarton Oaks, for example, or the Gulbenkian – and turned into a perpetual seminar for Byzantine studies. But these are only conditional hypotheses, depending on other sets of circumstances which may never arise. Surely the time has now come for the formulation of some tentative plans, and it would be comforting to think that the Greek Government had started some serious consideration of the question. This, so far as I have been able to discover, they have not done.

Meanwhile, we can only wait for the eventual collapse, and try to assess the extent of the inevitable loss. There will be many, doubtless, who will feel that Athonite monasticism is nothing but what Montalembert called "*une grande et lamentable aberration*" and will shed few tears at the disappearance of Europe's greatest stronghold of superstition and prejudice. Fertile land is in short supply, they will point out; why should a poor country like Greece allow over a hundred square miles of outstandingly rich soil to lie virtually untended for the sake of a few doddering monks who seldom if ever leave the confines of their own monasteries? If they have movables of value, send them to Athens or Salonica. If the buildings are worth keeping, turn them into museums and throw them open to the tourist trade. For the rest, the sooner the developers get to work the better.

On rational grounds these arguments will be hard to answer; and Athos will, anyway, be gone past hope of recall. But others of us will feel differently. We shall remember the never-failing excitement of arriving at an unknown monastery just before sunset, and speculating on the warmth of the reception that

34
The sixteenth-century gate-tower of Karakallou

E

awaited us; we shall remember, too, the nights when we crossed a moonlit courtyard to the katholikon and listened, leaning back in our stalls, while those dark and shrouded figures, insubstantial as the shadows from which they emerged, exchanged the droning supplications of their liturgy back and forth across the echoing church, and the frescoed saints glowed and glimmered in the candle-light. We shall think of the mornings on the silent, sunlit beaches, and the evenings on these vertiginous balconies, gazing out over the sea, when we held one old monk after another spellbound with a comparison of the population figures of London and Paris, Tokyo and New York. If we are lucky we may even manage to capture, for a moment or two, that feeling of peace and serenity which is still, perhaps, the greatest single benediction that the Holy Mountain can confer. And we shall know full well that both Europe and the world have been diminished by the passing of a strange and splendid society – the monks of Athos, who have endured in an unbroken line for well over a thousand years and have continued to enshrine, until the very end, something of Byzantium.

AN ACCOUNT OF THE VISIT MADE BY THE AUTHORS AND A. COSTA IN 1964

RERESBY SITWELL

35
The Russian monastery of
St Pantaleimon

An account of the visit made by the authors and A. Costa in 1964

The monastic republic of the Holy Mountain is an autonomous protectorate that occupies a remote peninsula in northern Greece. Twenty "Ruling Monasteries" share government and own the land. In addition, a number of dependencies are to be found: some resemble the monasteries and others vary in size and appearance from small villages to the precarious cliff-dwellings of anchorites. A survival of the Byzantine way of living set in a landscape that has remained unchanged since antiquity.

We came to study the churches, libraries and treasures, and to record in photographs as much as the monks would permit. After three nights in Athens, where we obtained further letters of recommendation from the Greek Foreign Office to the Holy Synod and inspected the great exhibition of Byzantine art, we flew on to Salonica, toured its many ancient churches and next morning took the bus to Erissos on the narrow neck of land leading to Athos.

East of Salonica the road leaves the dull Macedonian plain and starts to climb, twist and turn into hilly, thickly wooded country that appears on the map as a broken hand with three fingers thrusting at the Aegean. The hand is Chalcidice and the fingers are Cassandra, Longos and Athos. Driving across the "knuckles" occasional glimpses confirm that the third and most easterly finger culminates in a mighty promontory, and this is the Holy Mountain. The bus stops just long enough for one to risk crayfish with Turkish coffee at the birthplace of Aristotle and meanders on, calling at a hamlet that specialises in *souvlakia* (suspect meat on skewers). Suddenly the road winds down to the sea-shore and comes to an

36
The sacristan at Karakallou displaying the relics of the monastery

abrupt halt on a spit of sand that acts as market square for the fishing village and forlorn resort of Erissos, bus terminal and last settlement this side of Athos. Ahead lie one or two farms, then the patterned agriculture itself ends and a tumble-down wall proclaims the strangest of all frontiers, beyond which no woman, eunuch, child or female animal may stray.

Should we gird ourselves up, shoulder our rucksacks and tramp over the isthmus, following the line of Xerxes' canal through the sand dunes to Prosphori, there to waste another night before catching the boat to Daphni, official port for Athos? Should we hazard displeasure of the ecclesiastical authorities and turn up, unannounced and without the all-important *Diamoniterion* or monkish pass-port, at the first monastery to be reached from this, the eastern coast of the penin-sula? A waiting *engazé*, or boat for hire, settled the problem and, while Costa bargained with the skipper and mate, we slung our impedimenta on board.

Turning round, we levelled the sights of our cameras at the little throng that pushed and waved us out to sea; the last women and children we should see until our return. Erissos and the rest of the world faded into the distance and a strange feeling of leaden melancholy and loneliness descended, as the boat struck across the bay to round a distant headland. We strained to see the Wall, but it seemed as illusory as the lost canal of Xerxes. Instead, a wild and mysterious coastline came in view and we became aware for the first time of the great forest that stretches nearly forty miles from end to end of Athos. One or two white-washed houses appeared but no inhabitants and, as we drew closer, we noticed that most of the buildings, whether designed as farms or fishermen's cottages or, in some instances, to resemble small villas were in a ruinous condition. Only the churches seemed to be kept in repair. A deserted country where the surviving population, we supposed, must live in absolute peace, undisturbed by the tele-phone or any other manifestation of modern noise, save for their own church bells and the infernal din of our diesel engine.

We rounded the cape. Already it was getting cooler and the shadows on the farther shore obscured the landscape and gave it an even more sombre aspect. Two hours passed before we neared a diminutive port. On an islet hard by stood the prosperous abode of an archimandrite, or so we surmised, backed on the seaward side by remains of medieval fortifications. Drawing in to the landing-stage we saw several little houses showing signs of habitation and from one a strange figure emerged, sporting sandals, jeans and bush shirt beneath the thick beard and conical hat of an Orthodox priest. Shouts of welcome revealed that he was a Greek, but harbour-master of Chilandar, the Serbian monastery. We landed and immediately began the first of many lengthy and, alas, to me completely incomprehensible discussions in which Costa, our spokesman, recounted our various identities, origins, reputed faiths and current professional activities. Smiling benignly, our new friend bade us follow and clambered up the stairs of his control tower to a curious chamber that combined the functions of look-out, office, kitchen and potting shed. Two unexpected sights confronted us: a telephone and a bevy of hens out of the back window, evidences of compromise between tradition and expediency. The harbour-master picked up the receiver and, after a long pause and an even longer conversation of which most anxiously we awaited the outcome, he turned to us and intimated that the good fathers would make us welcome. Despite our unseemly lack of documentation we were to be afforded food and shelter for the night. "Order the muleteers to saddle the strangers' effects," the guest-master had commanded, "and tell the travellers to hasten on to us before we have the gates closed at sunset against all-comers."

Three of the sleekest mules from the drove grazing behind the arsenal of the little port were made ready while we took leave of the harbour-master and of the crew of our *engazé*, who opted to doss down on their craft for the night.

We set off past the hen coops and kitchen garden of the sailor hermit over the only flat expanse of ground we were to encounter during our whole itinerary, along a sandy track that led through meadows to the forest edge. Now that the noise of the engine had ceased the only sounds were the hum of insects, the patter of hooves from the mules that followed and the distant murmur of the sea. We came to a bend and the forest stretched out before us. On one side was a hill crowned with cypress trees and scant traces of building, and nearer to hand, a ILL. 3   ruined tower girt with scaffolding. This we were to learn was the Tower of Milutin built, according to one legend, by a Serbian queen at the nearest point to her son's monastery so that from the top of it she could gaze in the direction of Chilandar.

On we trudged down the forest glade, skirting a dried-up watercourse, to the increasing chorus of song-birds and the rhythm of a myriad cicadas. In a clearing appeared a grove of ancient olive trees, some of their gnarled bodies festooned with wild roses. Bay trees, myrtle, fig and arbutus mingled with shrubs of oleander and, among the profusion of wild flowers, the bright hues of delphinium and valerian caught our attention. The track widened as we reached a clump of cypresses and a rusty iron railing that guarded a humble red-brick shrine: indifferent frescoes were unwanted proof of dedication, for all around stood madonna lilies.

ILL. 4

Over a low wall beside the road, vineyards and plots of vegetables heralded the monastery, still hidden among the trees. Gradually the enormous edifice and a complex of smaller buildings were sighted, like a monster whale with full supporting cast. Grassy cobbles led to a gatehouse with arcaded upper storey and at the thickly studded doors we were met by a servant in shirt-sleeves and green baize apron. While the mules were being unloaded, we stumbled through the cavernous entrance passage into the courtyard which lay splayed before us in shape of a fan. Occupying the centre of the stage in architecture as well as in the life of the monastery stood the great church or *katholikon*, the finest exterior on the Holy Mountain, its lines enhanced by the striped effect of bricks laid in alternate courses of grey and red. Dominating the background, an immense tower of stone with square-cut machicolations and tiled roof in Central European mode suggested the haunt of robber barons rather than the last refuge of holy men. All the surrounding buildings seemed of later date but harmonised with the church, as it were in loyal display of house colours, including the smallest, a jaunty little baroque well-head, complete with its own cupola and flanked by two cypresses, one of perfect proportions and gigantic stature.

ILL. 22

A monk interrupted our thoughts to point to our baggage and to a huge, projecting wing designed in the uniform stripes and housing a staircase of cyclopean dimensions. Up and up we climbed, first on stone and then on timber treads, heaving our burdens to the window on each successive flight with the excuse of re-examining the view, until at last we reached the top floor and the smiling countenance of the guest-master. He led us into an ante-room, helped us out of our rucksacks and ushered us to a row of Windsor chairs. Now it was the turn

37
On the shore at Xeno-
phontos

38
Costa and Reresby in the
guest-room at Xenophontos

39 (overleaf)
At the Grand Lavra

of John Julius, who addressed the delighted Serb in his native tongue, only to find he had acquired tolerable English during five years as an engineer in Manchester before hearing the call! He was aged about forty with the handsome looks of the Dinaric race, tall and slender with finely chiselled features and a thick, black beard that augmented his magisterial bearing. Twenty-five monks remained in the house, of which the name – Chilandar – might be taken from its original foundation for one thousand inmates, but high hopes were held that permission would be granted for a draft of ten more novices from the homeland. He made excuses to leave us for a few minutes to attend to other duties and we were free to examine the wall of melodramatic portraits from the stormy history of the Southern Slavs and admire the potted plants trained around the window frames.

The guest-master returned, carrying a silver tray on which were displayed the local variants of the traditional Athonite welcome: for each of us a tumbler of water, a smaller glass that proved to contain slivovitz, a cup of Turkish coffee and a saucer of jam.

Nervously, we watched each other observe the correct procedure. First we gulped the slivovitz, then drank the water, next discovered that the jam was a superb concoction of quinces, and each asked and received a second helping from our indulgent host before sipping the Turkish coffee as final act in the ritual. By now candles were lit and we groped our way to a clean dormitory with four brass bedsteads. Communal life had begun. After a rather desperate kit inspection, the guest-master reappeared to announce supper; we followed in trepidation. A new and rather disturbing feature was now revealed: despite the varying degrees in which property is held in common in at least the stricter, cenobitic, houses, a strong class distinction is practised in treatment of guests. Our worthy muleteer and one or two other fleeting figures had been relegated to a different mess-room and, presumably on the strength of our brand-new rucksacks, all purchased the previous week at the Lost Property Office in Piccadilly, we were deemed to be neither workers nor peasants and were teamed up with two architects, officials of Marshal Tito's Ministry of Works. To my joy one spoke French. The food, as expected, was cold and included beans, but was palatable and adequate: boiled fish and roast potatoes with salads of onion and cucumber,

40
Father Jeremias at the
Russian skete of St Andrew

41
The sacristan at Vatopedi

washed down with strange but excellent apricot-tinted wine. Our host did not eat with us but remained to supervise, and during the meal we learned much from him and from our two new companions of the history and antiquities of the monastery.

Chilandar was founded by two Serbian princes, the Grand Zhupan Stephen Nemanja and his second son, at the end of the twelfth century. The son left court secretly, came to Athos and took his vows as the monk Sava. Eventually discovering his son's whereabouts and all other emissaries having failed to dislodge him, the distraught father made his own way to Athos but, so impressed was he by the monastic life that he resigned his throne to another son and became a monk at Vatopedi, taking the name of Simeon. Later father and son obtained permission from the former king's father-in-law, the Emperor Alexius III Angelus, to found their own monastery. Simeon died at Chilandar but Sava returned to become Archbishop of Serbia.

A century later another Serbian king, Stephen Milutin, rebuilt the katholikon and constructed the great tower, all that survived a disastrous fire in 1722. Milutin is also credited with the tower described on our way to Chilandar. Slavs have always predominated at this monastery, but at times Bulgarians have outnumbered Serbs.

After supper we attended compline for an hour or so and witnessed the glories of the Slavonic mass, sung by a handful of old men with cracked voices but with all the fervency of intonation that has re-echoed from these walls every night for seven centuries. As the service progressed with manifold repetition, priest and choir moved back and forth and the plan of the building was revealed.

From the porch or *pronaos* we entered the western door and passed through two vestibules, or *narthices*, the second one a few steps higher than the first, noticing the exterior doors to north and south, a special feature of Serbian architecture which obviates the clutter of side-chapels that often spoil the symmetry of Greek churches. On we tiptoed into the nave and stood, or rather hung, in the stalls as the choir in the apses to left and right gave alternating responses to the priest intoning from the dark recesses of the sanctuary. Presently he appeared, robed in splendour at the little gate in the centre of the *iconostasis*, that great rood-screen in Orthodox churches that shields the Holy of Holies from the gaze of the faithful. We tried to make out details of the frescoes around and above us by the light diffused from candles set in the choir stalls and in the mighty chandelier, the *corona*, hanging by chains below the dome. And then three candles were lowered by pulleys, ignited by taper and raised to the very top of the iconostasis, lighting the cross on high.

We followed back to the *exonarthex*, or outer vestibule, the monks chanting all the way. Every now and then a glimmer of meaning came through: the universal tones of "*Kyrie eleison*" or the hushed pleading of "*Gospodi, pomiluy*" (Lord have mercy). One by one we crept off to bed, across the moonlit courtyard and up the echoing staircase.

I woke that night to the sound of nightingales and jackals, and to reflect on the less congenial company of other dormitories long ago. Despite the beauty and excitement of that first day on Athos I was home-sick. Nights of anguish in the barrack-room and the earlier, stark horror that followed arrival at boarding-school flooded back. Jackal voices seemed to mock: "You'll have to get a move on when you get to Esphigmenou" . . . "We'll give Vatopedi a licking at footer."

Next morning we were up at dawn. After breakfast on the same commons as cocktails the previous evening, including the slivovitz, and a first timid assault on the "long drop", we rushed down to waylay the priest as he left church and beg him to unlock the treasury. However, the poor old man was exhausted and refused point-blank, to the obvious distress of the guest-master who explained that nowadays Chilandar could muster but two priests, fully ordained and qualified to hold mass and entrusted with the keys: one had the honour to serve at Karyes this year as *Protepistates*, or head of the entire community, and thus to his colleague fell the duty of every service, day and night. So we missed various holy relics and likewise were denied the library with its collection of medieval Slavonic and Byzantine manuscripts. As consolation we were given free rein to photograph church and refectory, both liberally covered with wall paintings in the style and content of medieval work, and vestiges of the original frescoes could be discerned in the katholikon. However, the chiefest glory revealed to us by daylight was the coloured marble floor of the church in *opus Alexandrinum*, dating from the original foundation. On a pillar near the sanctuary we admired the curious *Panaghia Trikheiroussa*, the icon of the Virgin-with-Three-Hands. In a corner we found the tomb of St Simeon with a painting of the Saint on his death-bed, against a background of medieval architecture, but dated 1780. From the tomb grows a vine supported by a trellis on the wall outside and credited with strange properties. The grapes are dried and given to childless couples to render their union fruitful; however, any male offspring thus engendered is bound to end his days as a monk at Chilandar.

It was time to leave and, if I have lingered overlong in trying to describe this first monastery, that is because of its peculiar beauty and strangeness, unlike any previous experience, different in character and in many particulars from sister foundations, and yet typical of all. So we made our farewells and began the trek back to the arsenal.

Our next port of call was the abbey of Esphigmenou. Most picturesque is the approach from the sea that laps against its bleak stone walls and fine views are obtained from the hills around. The name "Tight-Girdled One" does not merely refer to its cramped position but is a pointer to the austerity that prevails within.

ILL. 2

Today is the Feast of Esphigmenou and the Greek flag proudly flutters in the breeze atop the keep. We land quickly and are rushed through into the court-yard and up the steps of the church in time for the spectacle described by John Julius of "the abbot in full sail, billowing in awful solemnity from *katholikon* to refectory. . . ." (See page 44.)

ILL. 9

Close on the abbot's heels surge a pack in full cry of the inmates of Esphigmenou under his immediate care and guidance, hermits from outlying dependencies and representatives from other monasteries, followed by civilians led by police in baggy, pale green uniforms from the lonely station at neighbouring Vatopedi, one or two tourists, lay servants and peasants from the mainland, all in shirt-sleeves and sweaters, making a shabby contrast to the monks in their "Sunday best", the habits of senior brethren revealing dark-red sashes and cabbalistic signs.

Latecomers, gatecrashers, beggars and godless opportunists, all are welcome to join the monks and faithful in the banquet. The guest-master and assistants scurry round filling places at the long trestle tables, the good fathers sitting along the walls facing their guests in the middle. The monk on picquet duty climbs the

42
A capital of the *Old Katholikon* at Xenophontos

stairs up to his rostrum and starts to read the appointed scriptures for the day, and the feast begins.

Pewter plates and mugs, and wine decanters of generous proportions, are laid with slabs of bread and eating irons by every place alongside the first course, cold soup. Visions come to mind of *Vichyssoise* and *Crème Germiny* that might tempt St Anthony Abbot himself, but the reality is gruel, a liquid substance in which thick, coagulated lumps of homogeneous matter are suspended. In our efforts to show appreciation to our hosts and conceal our true feelings Costa, John Julius and I make valiant inroads, assisted by the good red wine, turning discreetly every now and then to compare progress. The lector drones on.

A line of serving-men bring round the *entrée*, an unidentified fish of molluscous provenance; soft white flesh still on the bone, steamed beforehand and cooled by steeping in oil of acrid pungency, much to the taste of my neighbour opposite who presses me to share a spare portion. In vain I beg Costa to explain I am on a diet, but by this time the monk is at grips with his limpet, spraying the juice over his beard. Sheep's cheese, hard-boiled eggs and oranges from Salonica complete the fare. We quaff our wine, nervously whisper thanks and withdraw to explore our surroundings.

Beautiful as is the setting of Esphigmenou, the architecture is disappointing on closer view. The same stripes are in vogue as at Chilandar but, apart from the katholikon with its smart, white marble *pronaos* and the refectory, both dated 1810, all other buildings betray the heavy, if competent, hands of the mid-nineteenth century. The main and most unexpected curiosity is the magnificent embroidery of mysterious Napoleonic origin now used as a hanging in the church and much prized by the monks.

The monastery is one of the oldest on the Holy Mountain and has always been one of the poorest. Here in 1821 the leading monks of Athos assembled under their "Captain", Emmanuel Papas of Serres, to take part in the Greek War of Independence with disastrous results to the community. Russian interest was long attracted here by its close proximity to the cave of an early ascetic, St Anthony of Kiev, and generous contributions would arrive, often followed by attempts at political interference.

However, if the monks are poor by material standards, apart from relics and

manuscripts, they are rich in the spirit. We were to find cenobitic monks humbler and kinder as a rule, always pleased to offer hospitality, display their treasures or, even after a whole night in vigil, to show us their living-quarters or pose
in groups by the fountain or the lovingly tended roses.

ILLS 7, 8 & 20

Early that afternoon we took a walk over an ancient footbridge to a neighbouring hill crowned by a deserted hermitage with panoramic views of Esphigmenou. Later we re-embarked for Vatopedi.

ILL. II

The Holy, Venerable, Imperial and Patriarchal Monastery of the Boy and the
Bramble Bush is the second in seniority and the most imposing of all. Legend
derives the name from the shipwrecking of the youthful Arcadius, first of the
separate line of Emperors of the East who, caught in a storm and calling on the
Virgin, was miraculously landed in a thorn bush on these shores. Historical
evidence, however, alludes to a foundation by three brothers, citizens of Adri-
anople, in the year 972.

High above lay the ruins of the short-lived Theological School of Athos and,
below in parkland stretching down to the sea, were ranged the walls, towers and
fortifications of Vatopedi. We landed, paid off the *engazé* and made our way
past the arsenal and up the hill to the gatehouse. To one side lay a moat of running water and, set apart on a raised platform stood the first of many gazebos or
kiosks, airy pavilions constructed of wood with benches and hand-rail on
three sides and tiled roof above, where the monks sit and contemplate in the
cool of the evening. We entered under the baldacchino porch and came up
to the porter's lodge. Here we became aware of the more worldly and practical
approach to life that characterises Vatopedi, the only house on the Holy Mountain that accepts the Gregorian calendar and keeps 'Frankish' time with the rest of
the world. Beneath the notice-board reminding tourists of the religious nature of
the precincts and the need to observe decorum in behaviour and apparel, was a
little shop: postcards, maps, guide-books, paper and pencils, torches and tinned
foods were displayed, together with products of Athonite craftsmanship; immense wooden bowls of doubtful application and cumbersome bulk, cunningly
wrought walking-sticks of ancient design but varnished to the hideous brightness
of a cuckoo clock, and butter moulds reproducing simple patterns of crosses,
primitive religious scenes and the emblem of the double-headed eagle, insignia

of the Byzantine Empire and of the Orthodox Church, later affected by so many
parvenu monarchies now vanished. I settled for an eagle, stuffed it to the bottom
of my kitbag and strolled on through the usual tortuous passage into the monastery.

ILL. 12

The greatest courtyard on Athos, as at Cambridge, is the pride of the most
imposing but not the senior foundation. But how different from Trinity with its
flat contours and sober English masonry is the riot of shape and colour that
confronts the newcomer to Vatopedi! First, we are on a sharply rising slope
paved, as another visitor has described, with pebbles that ripple away into the
distance. And then, instead of one great fountain in the centre, a whole jumble
of buildings that once included twelve towers and sixteen churches bewilder the
eyes. Nor is it their number and complexity, their variety in styles and dates
over a thousand years that so amaze, but the fantastic wealth of colour. Mellowed
brick and weathered stone contend and stripes in places are the rage, but every
shade and tone from the blue of the firmament above to the grit-grey of the
pebbles under foot yields to the vivid red of the katholikon, painted to sym-
bolise the Saviour's Blood. Rust red, crimson or incarnadine are many churches
on Athos and this is their awful secret. Here at Vatopedi the katholikon is tucked
away into a corner of the vast interior space, but its presence is emphasised by the
matching paint on clock tower, refectory and other buildings. Knowing it and
the library to contain some of the most interesting and historic treasures we could
hope to see, we clambered up the outside stair to the rather depressing guest
quarters, in order to check-in and enquire when visits might be made.

ILLS 15, 16 & 50

Interest in the katholikon starts with the frescoes in the porch, protected against
the sun by a makeshift arrangement of flapping sheets. Scenes such as the Annunciation, Nativity and Adoration of the Magi flank the entrance of fine bronze
doors between columns of the tenth century; one steps into the *exonarthex* and
familiar episodes from the Life and Passion of Our Lord emerge in the dim
light. Over the next doorway is a renowned mosaic of the eleventh century:
below a semi-circular inscription dedicating the church to the Annunciation is
the seated figure of Christ in Majesty between Mary and John the Baptist. Panels
on either side depict the Angel Gabriel and the Virgin, and other mosaics of the
same subject appear elsewhere. The interior is complicated by the subdivision of

the inner narthex into *mesonyktikon* and *lite*. In the first of these lies a tomb containing the remains of two imperial benefactors, Manuel II Palaeologus and John VI Cantacuzene and from the *lite* open side-chapels to St Demetrius of Salonica on the north and to St Nicholas on the south. The frescoes are continued throughout the church on every available wall and vault, culminating in the Last Supper, Crucifixion, Resurrection and Transfiguration; they date from 1312, belong to the so-called "Macedonian" school but were restored at the end of the eighteenth century. From the floor of *opus Alexandrinum* in the nave rise four monolithic columns of granite that support the dome. Much fine woodwork exists, particularly the superb iconostasis; there are doors of inlaid ivory and reading desks of inlaid pearl. The general feeling is in marked contrast to the exterior: the subdued light on the rich details within imbues a strong sense of mystery.

The monk in charge of the treasury came, by a stroke of luck, from the same ILLS 18, 32 & 41 peninsula as Costa's forbears, a circumstance that militated more than any argument in our favour from bishop, professor or government official. So we were taken behind the iconostasis into the *bema* or sanctuary and permitted to examine and photograph at leisure the Virgin of the Sacristan, the inextinguishable candle that neither time, nor raiding Saracens, nor even the well in which it and the Madonna were hidden can ever quench, the Cross of Constantine and a host of smaller icons. Silver-gilt reliquaries encasing grisly remains of saints were produced, a pair of minute reliefs in steatite, a composition marble similar to soapstone, and three exquisite portable mosaics, miniature icons of the Crucifixion, Our Lady with St Anne, and St John Chrysostom. Finally, the greatest treasures of all were unlocked: set in gold and precious stones were portions of the Holy Cross, the Reed and the Girdle of the Virgin. This last is a ribbon of reddish-brown camel hair, presented to Vatopedi by the fourteenth-century Serbian Prince Lazar Hrebljanovich and long sent round as a cure to cities smitten with the plague. Before leaving we examined the miraculous icon of the Virgin which bled when struck by an angry deacon who had missed his supper; the offending and unwitherable hand that dealt the sacrilegious blow is preserved in a box below the picture.

Situated in the conventional place opposite the west door of the katholikon is the refectory, built in 1785 and decorated with panels of frescoes but seldom ILLS 21 & 22 used as this is an idiorrhythmic monastery where the monks eat alone. Near by stand the fine clock-tower, dating from 1427, the oldest on the mountain, and an elaborate version of the usual *phiale*, or fountain; a double row of columns support the dome over a marble basin.

The library contains over six hundred manuscripts and many early printed books, besides interesting Greco-Roman remains, fragments of statues and vases that have been dug up on the monastery's estates or fished out of the sea. In glass cases are Ptolemy's *Geography*, *chrysobuls* of the emperors signed in the imperial scarlet, and a copy of the Gospels written by the Emperor John Cantacuzene, the friend and supporter of the Hesychasts, who retired here as the monk Joasaph after his futile usurpation and is buried in the tomb we have noticed. Also on show is the cup presented by the Emperor's son Manuel, Despot of Mistra (see page 91). It is interesting to read the opinion of this item by John Julius in his section of this book and compare that with the fulsome description by Robert Byron in *The Station*, published in 1928, he writes: "In the whole collection one object stands alone. This is the cup bestowed on the monastery by Manuel Cantacuzenus, son of the Emperor of that name, who was despot of Mistra from 1349 to 1380. Standing about 10 inches high, it consists of a broad bowl of transparent, gold-flecked jasper, yellow, dark green, and red, which is mounted on a thick octagonal stalk of silver-gilt. From a bulge in the centre of this, two rhythmic tapering dragons spring off at a tangent, until, taking an acute-angled turn, they come to rest upon the metal rim, wings folded, heads supported by little pairs of clutching claws. The base is also octagonal. And on every other facet are chased the circular monograms of the donor (to read): "Manuel Despot Cantacuzene Palaeologus." For my part, I must confess deep admiration for what I consider to be a beautiful object, although I am aware that historical associations may press upon judgement, as clearly happened to Robert Byron on many occasions. I would far sooner possess this chalice than many of the masterpieces attributed to Benvenuto Cellini, notwithstanding my abiding enjoyment of his memoirs and an inborn love of the Italian Renaissance.

Next morning we engaged the services of a muleteer, who saddled our effects on to a handsome beast and led us up the mountain path to Karyes and respectability, we hoped, in the form of official sanction for our wanderings.

F

The wooded demesne of the great monastery merged imperceptibly into scrub and, in turn, thickets of arbutus, boxwood, myrtle and judas trees gave way to dense forest of ilex, Spanish chestnut and pine. We laboured uphill, becoming painfully conscious that the paths which dissect the Holy Mountain, if devised in some way for the convenience of brute beasts of burden, are not intended to facilitate the passage of two-legged pilgrims but to add to their penance and discomfort. An endless procession of knife-edged stones, tightly laid together, seemed to lead ever onwards and upwards, and thick vegetation hemmed in the track on either side to rule out any short cuts. We passed the ruined Theological College and tramped on, pausing now and then for breath and to glance once again at the little harbour and cluster of buildings far below. Occasionally we spied lonely *kellia*, little hermitages tucked away in the forest, each with its beehive dome to indicate a chapel. We reached the crest of the ridge and trundled on, marvelling at the sylvan landscape of luxuriant timber on every side, now the sole source of income for most of the monasteries. By a stone fountain with a water trough under a great lime tree we stopped to picnic. I lit my portable gas cooker and produced *bisque de homard* from a packet, which we followed with processed cheese and Bath biscuits, washed down with Nescafé. Two hours later we reached the outskirts of Karyes, passing on our left the immense and ruinous Russian *skete* of St Andrew.

Nuts, to be precise, hazel-nuts, is the meaning of the name Karyes, and very strange is the atmosphere of this capital without women or children. Two cafés, three post offices – but no bank – the lay police station and six or seven shops, selling mainly groceries or souvenirs, comprise the two streets that lead to the *Protaton*, the foremost church in Athos, and behind looms the ugly modern building with imposing staircase and hefty arcading that houses the *Holy Epistasia*, the governing hierarchy. One or two lesser shrines with the dwellings of guardians and devotees are conspicuous, and the rest of the village consists of the *konakia*, or embassies of the twenty Sovereign Monasteries to the federal authority.

We made our way to the corner café shrouded with a vine next to the cobbler monk's shop, ordered Turkish coffee and took stock of the situation. A beady-eyed monk was munching cherries out of a bag; above him hung a First World

War poster of Messrs Clemenceau, Lloyd George and Woodrow Wilson. In a corner sat a defiant and verminous figure in rags, with matted hair and beard, and cumbrous wooden crutches: while opposite this crippled prophet slouched the lonely and disconsolate figure of a visiting *savant*, inarticulate, overspent and, in these surroundings every bit as pathetic as his neighbour. Outside in the square before the *Protaton* the tinkling of little bells and clatter of hooves on the cobbles announced a long mule-train bearing hay. A scabrous youth appeared with the coffee and explained that he ran the place with his father "during the season", and indeed the establishment became a focal point during the rest of our visit, supplying the same function in our lives as the Bar of the *Ritz* has done for past generations of tourists in Paris or the Buttery of the *Hibernia* for people in Dublin. We left our belongings in charge of the management, who warned us not to whistle in the Street of the Holy Ghost and, as the government offices were closed, we went first to the Protaton.

The square in the centre of Karyes resembles a shapeless parade-ground and its existence proves that ecclesiastical councils are no less tidy-minded and destructive than their lay municipal counterparts; a medley of picturesque buildings and market stalls have been swept away in recent years to provide a vacuum like that made by Mussolini for his approach to St Peter's.

The *Protaton* is not only the *foremost* church on the Holy Mountain, but is unusual, if not unique, among Byzantine churches in that it has a wooden roof and no dome, and displays an "open plan" with the narthex leading straight through to the nave, thus gaining in western eyes a simplicity of design at the expense of the mystery we have noted elsewhere. The origins of the building go back to the very beginnings of the Athonite community; a long-vanished monastery is believed to have existed in its immediate vicinity and an earlier church on this site is by tradition one of those which were destroyed by order of the Emperor Michael VIII, the re-conqueror of Constantinople in 1261 and first of the Palaeologue dynasty, in his efforts to enforce compromise with Rome. The present construction was in part rebuilt at the expense of the Rumanian prince John Bogdan, Voivode of Moldavia, in 1508, and the exterior has been refaced in recent years. The extensive frescoes are attributed to Panselinos, who seems to occupy in medieval Greek painting much the same standing but vague achievement as Praxiteles in ancient sculpture. Moreover, whereas the approximate dates and some of the works of the great Athenian are established beyond reasonable doubt, the life and times of Panselinos may have occurred at any period between the thirteenth and seventeenth centuries A.D. However, the paintings in the Protaton, although much restored in the sixteenth century and later, are now generally accepted as belonging to the early fourteenth century and so contemporary with original work at Vatopedi and Chilandar.

The frescoes are arranged in four tiers around the walls. The first row, just below the roof, portrays the ancestors of Christ; the second and third are the finest and depict scenes from the lives of Christ and of the Virgin, continuing with portraits of saints that end in the fourth and lowest section with the patrons of the individual monasteries. The strong characterisation of the faces, displaying emotions of a Slav intensity seldom found in Greek Byzantine art, and the skilful treatment of draperies and varied use of perspective in background architecture are most remarkable in the *Washing of the Disciples' Feet*, *Jesus on the Mount of Olives*, and the *Nativity* and *Presentation* of the Virgin, all to be found in the south transept.

The most famous of all the icons of Athos is preserved here, the Virgin known as "*Axión estin*" ("*Worthy it is*"), in the place of honour at the back of the sanctu-   ILL. 33
ary. The sacristan was relating how the Archangel Gabriel appeared before this icon on June 11, 980, and prompted an absent-minded novice how to preface a hymn with the words "Worthy it is to magnify thee, Mother of God", when our attention was distracted by a loud clattering. In burst the ragged cripple from the café. Swinging his remaining leg at speed with powerful strokes, he implanted a smacking kiss on every icon within reach until he came to the "*Axión estin*", cast aside his crutches and heaved his mangled frame on to the ledge below the image. In a trice he had clambered down, picked up his crutches and hobbled off. No time need be wasted on prayer or supplication; he must make haste to the next hallowed place while he had the strength. We had witnessed a classic scene from the Christian middle ages, and yet I had seen wild-eyed holy men in sackcloth and ashes rush in like manner from one Hindu shrine to another, in particular near the burning *ghats* on the River Baghmati, by the golden temple of   44
Shiva at Pashupatinat in Nepal. Again, the prolonged contemplation of the   A monk of Xenophontos

navel still practised by latter-day Hesychasts has obvious parallels in Hindu ascetic teaching. Outside in the street the projecting eaves and timber-strutted galleries recalled Himalayan architecture, and yet how far is Katmandu with its bloody sacrifices of bulls and its Living Goddess!

We made our way to the civilian police station, where a sad-looking young man stamped our papers and wished us good luck, recrossed the square and mounted the steps to the Holy Epistasia. Ecclesiastical gendarmes appeared, bearded in the approved monkish fashion, and wearing battle-dress of celestial blue with forage-caps bearing silver badges of the double-headed eagle. We handed in our passports and applications, and the inevitable cups of Turkish coffee were brought to us to while away the time that our fate was in balance. Eventually our passports were returned, and inside each was the long-awaited and ever-to-be-cherished *Diamoniterion*, calling on the Sovereign Monasteries to afford us free board and lodging as the statutes prescribe and requesting that we be shown *and allowed to photograph* churches, icons and treasures. By an oversight, this last and most important clause had been omitted from mine and, in order to speed rectification, the gendarme had borrowed back John Julius's document to copy; as a result of further misunderstanding I am on record for all

ILL. 62

time as that rarest of aristocrats, an *uncreated* Greek viscount (*ipokomos*).

We returned triumphantly to the café and celebrated with high tea of fried eggs, bread and honey, washed down with *retsina* and more Turkish coffee. The monk was still munching cherries and eyed us curiously. Later we were to learn that this most idiorrhythmic of ecclesiastics had cornered all the tin-openers on the Holy Mountain. We ended by buying a large bag of cherries which stood us in good stead and, as sunset was drawing near, we set off for Koutloumousiou, the nearest monastery and only ten minutes' walk from the capital over a series of wooden stiles past orchards and vegetable gardens, near a mountain torrent.

The abbey of Koutloumousiou owes its outlandish name to its founder, a converted Turkish prince. The son of Azeddin II Kai-Kobad (1245–57), thirteenth and last effective Sultan of Iconium of the Seljuk dynasty, his mother was a Christian and he became reconciled to her faith, took the name of Constantine and died here in 1268. The principle icon, that of the *Dreadful Presentation*, exchanges visits with the *Axión estin* at the *Protaton* every Easter. The tower of

the monastery dates from the early sixteenth century and the church, dedicated   ILL. 26
to the Transfiguration, was rebuilt a few years later by Roumanian generosity
effected on this occasion by a prince of the Bassarab family. Since then Koutloumousiou has been as poor in history as in wealth and numbers; disastrous
fires occurred in 1767, 1856 and 1870 and the remaining inmates of this picturesque but shabby building can be counted on the fingers of two hands.

We arrived just in time before "lock-up", and an amiable but very dirty
youth showed us and the cripple who had reappeared to the guest quarters.
Beyond that no attempt was made in the way of entertainment. We dined off
the cherries and *retsina* on a most precarious balcony overhanging the courtyard
and red katholikon. The highlight of our visit, however, was the unexpected
luxury of individual bedrooms with basin and cold-water tap, and showers and
lavatories on the floor below. Alas, the condition of the latter was such as might
inhibit the natural functions for life. The millenary celebrations in 1963 had
occasioned these modern innovations to help accommodate the large numbers
of visiting clergy and laity. That night I nearly gassed myself by unnecessary use
of insecticide.

Early next day we were back in the café at Karyes, as were the monk, the
cripple and the Russian professor. From the capital and over the central ridge of
the peninsula to the port of Daphni there now runs a dirt road of recent construction, greatly abhorred by monks and visitors of conservative disposition,
but used by everyone as passengers of *the motor-coach*, (registration number AO 1).[1]
Another, more primitive, and most terrifying track takes *the lorry* (registration
number AO 2) to the monastery of Iveron, nearest point on the east coast to which
we elected to return. So, after breakfast and a maddening delay of three hours
spent in writing postcards and visiting the beautiful little chapel of the *Pro-*
dromos, or *Forerunner*, i.e. St John the Baptist, kept by a kindly old Father
Photios, we climbed aboard the lorry and risked life, limb and rucksack in a   ILL. 31
pell-mell rush down the mountainside.

Iveron, Monastery of the Iberians – not of the Spaniards but of the Georgians –
boasts a very early foundation with the most exotic origins of all. The Georgians,
it may be noted, were second only to the Armenians among nations to adopt

[1] The letters "AO" are initials standing for "Aghion Oros" (Holy Mountain).

Christianity and have always remained in the Orthodox fold, unlike their neighbours who have steered a lonely and tragic course throughout history. For twelve centuries the various branches of the Bagratid dynasty struggled to maintain a precarious independence against Persians, Arabs, Turks and Tartars until they finally submitted to Russian rule at the beginning of the nineteenth century. During the early centuries after their conversion, however, there were times when the Georgians had to accept a measure of Byzantine influence in politics as well as in religion and this accounts for the presence a thousand years ago of imperial armies in the Caucasus and of "Iberian" monks on Athos. And, when these troops revolted under Bardas Sclerus against the Emperor Basil the Bulgar-slayer in the year 979, it was to the Holy Mountain that the Emperor's mother Theophano turned for help. Summoned from his Athonite retreat, the warrior monk Thornic, *né* Grdzelidze, returned to his native Georgia and, with the aid of his lieutenant, one Dchodchic, and 12,000 fellow-countrymen raised by David the *Curopalates*, put down the rebellion. Next year he retired once more to the Holy Mountain laden with booty and founded the monastery. The Empress sent workmen and sacred vessels for the church, and Thornic was joined in his new enterprise by a brother named Waraz-Watché and various other kinsmen, including his brother-in-law John Varasvatze and nephew Euthymius, who each succeeded him in turn as abbot. Euthymius made the first translation of the Bible into Georgian; shortly after his death the first katholikon was built by the monk George Mthatsmidel with money provided by the Georgian King Bagrat IV (1027–72).

Since these illustrious beginnings Iveron has been destroyed time and again by "Latin" crusaders, Catalans and Palaeologi, infidel Turks, pirates, earthquakes and accidental fires, the most recent in 1865. Meanwhile the Greeks managed as long ago as the fourteenth century to winkle out the Georgians and all Iberian influence from the monastery, although gladly accepting financial help from that quarter on at least three subsequent occasions along with the usual generous contributions from Russia and Roumania. Finally, in a fit of xenophobic passion against the Tsar and all his subjects in 1913, they are alleged to have made a bonfire of the entire collection of Georgian manuscripts, including Abbot Euthymius' Bible.

The most interesting survival from the remote oriental origins of Iveron is the
method of keeping time. The rest of the community – except Vatopedi – adheres
to the Julian calendar and begins the day at sunset the previous evening, like the
Israelites, and is therefore thirteen and a half days late. Iveron counts the hours
from dawn and so preserves the ancient chronometry of fire worshippers.

The monastery stands a few hundred yards back from the sea on a little plain.
The present building is rectangular in shape and the entrance is through a colon-
naded porch in what F. W. Hasluck describes as "the modern barbarised classical
style"; Robert Byron is even ruder about the clock-tower as a "malformity of a
Wren steeple". As at Koutloumousiou, the church is a sixteenth-century survival   ILL. 29
of some of the fires and a few of the restorations. The frescoes date from 1593
to 1603; the exonarthex contains a gruesome series of martyrdoms and a beautiful
Dormition of the Virgin is painted in the traditional place over the doorway of
the *naos*, on the inside facing the iconostasis. There is a good marble floor as at
Vatopedi and Chilandar and much fine silver work in evidence. The most
remarkable feature is the elaborate ceramic tile decoration, reminiscent of the
Chapel of the Burning Bush at Mount Sinai, and ceramic plates are also used to
enliven the striped exterior.

The Chapel of the Virgin of the Gate (*Panaghia Portaïtissa*) enshrines an icon
attributed to St Luke. During the iconoclast régime at Constantinople it escaped
to sea, and after seventy years turned up off these shores but refused to land itself
except for "Gabriel the Iberian". Search was made for the worthy hermit; he
was unearthed from his lair and rushed out to meet the icon which, however,
would not settle down until housed in a chapel near the gate of the monastery
to be founded one hundred and fifty years later. The walls of the chapel are
decorated with curious portraits of Georgian princes, pious individuals connected with the history of the icon and pagan philosophers and historians pro-   46
phesying Christ: Plato, Aristotle, Thucydides, Plutarch and other figures from   Fresco of Christ Pantocrator
the schoolroom. In 1654 the monks secured the gift of much valuable farmland   in the central dome at
near Moscow in return for supplying Tsar Alexis with an exact copy of the icon   Docheiariou
to accomplish the miraculous cure of his illness; only consecrated water was used
to mix the paints and all work had to be done on Sundays and holy days in   47 (overleaf)
order to obtain maximum beneficial effect.   Dionysiou from the landward side

Iveron is a pillar of conservative Orthodoxy and seldom are its treasures displayed to strangers. To its credit it has a great tradition of missionary work and long maintained a leper colony. As long ago as 1886, the Reverend Athelstan Riley complains in *Athos or the Mountain of the Monks*, "We somehow missed seeing the relics", despite letters from the Oecumenical Patriarch and the status of one of his companions, the "Altogether Most Holy One Philotheos, by the Mercy of God the Most Reverend and Divinely Appointed Archbishop and Metropolitan of the Most Holy Metropolis of Xanthe and Christopolis, Highly Esteemed and Right Honourable". Riley confesses "We did not find these Iberian monks quite so pleasant as those at most of the other monasteries. They seemed to be of rather a lower class . . .!" Like our egregious Anglican forerunner and friends, however, we were admitted to the library which still retains much of interest, including a Greek classic printed at Eton in the seventeenth century that has so far ridden the storms of *Enosis*. We also admired a most beautifully embroidered tunic, complete with imperial eagle and said to have belonged to the Emperor John Tzimisces (969–76), who is depicted in this very garment in a fresco at the Grand Lavra. Tzimisces is an Armenian word and was given him to denote his short stature. According to George Finlay in *History of the Byzantine Empire from 716 to 1057*: "the name is written in a fearful manner, and with variations not adapted to render it euphonious . . . Chimishkik and Chumuskik". He was born at Chumushkazak or Tchemeschgedzek on the Euphrates.

In the ante-room of the guest quarters, with musty Victorian furniture and faded portraits of royalty from Tsars Alexis and Peter the Great to our own Edward VII, we were introduced to a fellow-visitor, a Greek theological student, hot-foot from a German university and about to enter an Orthodox seminary; he had the familiar glint in the eye and heavy tweed jacket of his ilk. After the customary tray we were led into a dining-room and each man was faced with two black olives, two anchovies *crossed in saltire* and two bowls of soup!

The absence of any looking-glass afforded John Julius and me the excuse to give up shaving next day; Costa persevered and, as soon as he, too, was ready, we made our usual present to the guest-master "for the church", said good-bye to the muscular Christian and joined Angelos, the new muleteer we had engaged

48
Dionysiou from the sea

at Karyes the previous morning with his three steeds outside the gate. We spent the next two days in march and counter-march, exploring the remaining monasteries on this section of the coast and, for some unaccountable reason Angelos alone and, for brief moments only Costa, who was suffering the agonies of lumbago, were permitted to ride. Our arrival and welcome at each monastery took after the pattern that follows.

The presence of alien figures panting up the hillside is felt, disturbing the idyllic peace of the forest tracts; lizards scurry into the undergrowth, a note of danger interludes the paean of the song-thrush and the jackals start up their weird and plaintive howl.

News travels even on Athos and, after a final excruciating climb and slither, the path turns and the vast form of a monastery appears, fortress-like and devoid of windows in the lower courses. In the tile-roofed gazebo by the entrance gate a group of tired and venerable old men with long beards and caftans make room for the strangers they seem to be expecting. After the phrases of welcome that propriety demands, the most active rises, straightens the bob of hair under his stove-pipe and disappears into the building. Long minutes of desultory conversation ensue until eventually the visitors are escorted to their quarters. Through the massive keep into the courtyard with a glimpse of the vermilion-painted church and then another climb begins; up immense staircases, along endless galleries and passages empty save for sparrows and house-martins and their nests, up further rickety stairs till at last the guest wing is reached. Here the suspicious but courtly presence of the guest-master is encountered and grubby fingers remove for scrutiny the *Diamoniterion* - monastic passport and splendid latter-day Byzantine document.

Pilgrims are invited to dispose of their rucksacks and a sitting-room with long rows of divans is indicated. Improbable lace curtains fringe the small windows, half hiding the incredible view of monkish flotsam and jetsam, tumbledown outbuildings, gardens and vineyards with virgin forest and sea beyond. The walls, brightly painted in primary colours, are hung with loyal but seldom up-to-date portraits of kings and queens and patriarchs, interspersed with the fierce likenesses of heroes of Greek independence and of earlier, shadowy, imperial personages. In the centre sits a table bedecked with a rug after the Dutch manner and supporting a visitors' book, vases of artificial flowers, inkstands and other paraphernalia grouped round a handsome oil lamp that defies the impotent electric fitting suspended above.

Enter the guest-master, now all smiles, having studied everyone's credentials and bearing aloft *the Tray*! . . . Conversation proceeds; one establishes whether this is a cenobion or a less strict, idiorrhythmic, house and how many or, rather, how few are its present inmates. Details of the history and treasures emerge and pilgrims are regaled with accounts of the icons and their miracles. At last dinner is announced and hunger and curiosity rise to a pitch. But, too often, high hopes raised by the tray of welcome are shattered by the horror and paucity of what Byron describes as a "travesty of a meal", usually vegetarian and stone cold.

Our way from Iveron led through a stretch of heathland ablaze with cytisus into the *Provata*, the *Garden of Athos*, plantations of woodland with scattered farms and vineyards. We stopped by the orchards and beehives of an ascetic retreat named Mylopotamou, and bathed among rocks at the delta of a mountain torrent. Later we traced the river inland to a ford. Here the mules were tethered, and we washed again in a rock pool, spread our picnic under the trees and hid from the mid-day sun. A party of monks on well-caparisoned mules came by and we exchanged greetings. The track zig-zagged, down to the shore, up to the cliff's edge and then inland. After an hour we forked right, passing a sinister and deserted Russian hermitage, overgrown with vines and oleander, to the hilltop convent of Philotheou.

The idiorrhythmic foundation of the hermit Philotheos is of problematic age and little interest. The Emperor Nicephorus Botaniates (1078–81) and the sixteenth-century Georgian princes Leontius and Alexander are honoured as principal benefactors, and the most venerated icon is a beautiful Madonna credited with the same navigational prowess as that at Iveron. The location in bucolic surroundings, one thousand feet above the sea and several miles inland, have protected Philotheou from the attacks of most enemies but not from the carelessness of its own monks; as elsewhere the church and refectory, both adorned with frescoes rather quaint than lovely, were witness to a general conflagration in 1781. Nevertheless, these circumstances in no way detract from the charm of the place or its occupants. During our brief call we noticed the cleanliness of the "usual offices" and, when offered the conventional hospitality, remarked on the *glyco* of a particularly delicious brand of cherry. This we enjoyed on a penthouse balcony overlooking the metal-roofed katholikon with a distant view over the forest and across the sea to the island of Thasos, where the monks held property in happier times. The guest-master posed for our cameras against a well-head outside the entrance, and we took our leave and returned by the same route until we met the coastal track again, and wandered on through groves of hazel and chestnut, the haunt of lizard and butterfly. As the sun began to sink over the mountain we reached our goal for the night, the cenobitic abbey of Karakallou, favoured retreat of Albanian and Epirote.

ILL. 30

The monks of Karakallou assert the most bizarre of origins for their ancient house, based on accidental similarity of names to one of the most vicious of tyrants before the demagogues and paranoiacs of our own age. Likewise, an ingenious Neapolitan princeling of antiquarian bent and candour of race has claimed one of his own ancestors as founder. Neither Caracalla nor Caracciolo are as plausible candidates for the honour as some obscure but eponymous ascetic of the Dark Ages. Whatever the truth of these matters, there was no doubt attached to the warmth of our reception.

While the muleteer and his beasts were taken in charge we admired our first clear view of the marble summit, briefly released from the enshrouding nimbus of clouds, and the luxuriant oleander and hydrangea along the outer walls. We were led through the crenellated gate-tower and, having dumped our belongings in a well-appointed dormitory, were accorded the preliminary civilities and shown over the church. This dates from 1535 and is due to the munificence of Peter Rareș, Hospodar of Moldavia and his *Protospatharios*, or First Swordsman. Apparently the official misappropriated his master's funds and on pain of death was obliged to complete the work at his own expense; in due course all was forgiven and eventually master and servant retired here, took their vows together, and both assumed the name Pachomius. The sacristan appeared, suitably invested, and exposed the relics on a trestle table in front of the iconostasis: the skulls of the Apostle Bartholomew and St Dionysius the Areopagite, the remains of a neomartyr, St Gideon, a converted Turk who suffered for his apostasy of

ILL. 34

ILL. 36

49
Xeropotamou

ΛΟΣ ΟΆΓ
ΒΑΙΟ · ΟΡΩ

ΜΚΆΡΙ · ΟΆΓΙΩ
ΜΕΟΣ ·

ΟC ΧΡΟ
ΤΟC ΪΠ
ΩΝ ΤΝ
ΕΡ Δ ΑΙ
Ν ΙΕ ΡΔΑ
ΒΙ ΔΕ·ΦCΕ
Ν Η ΤΪΑΜ
ΦΘΑΛΜΤ

Ι ΗΔΕΝ
ΒΛΠ ΤΕ
ΤΟΝ ΜΟ
ΝΧ ΟΝ
Ο ΥΤΩ
Ο ΓΕΛΩ
C ΚΑΙ Η
ΠΑΡΡΗ
CΙΑ ....

Ν ΕΛΓ
ΜΟΥΟ
ΤΚΡΗ
ΦΥΡΗ
Ο ΥΟ
CΚΕ Τ Ο
Τ Ο

Islam and was chopped to pieces by order of the Pasha of Thessaly in the year 1818, and another portion of the True Cross. We returned to our quarters.

Hospitality seemed to have no bounds once the former parachutist *maître-d'hôtel* discovered that we all of us had also known and loved Lizzie Lezard, a brave and comic South African who had served as liaison officer with the Greek Army in North Africa. We were hurriedly transferred to the patriarchal suite, complete with lavatory and pink "loo"-paper. A most amiable young Cypriot, evidently nicknamed "Makarios", replenished our glasses and showed us into a small dining-room of engaging oval shape, painted the duck-egg blue and pigeon white of the Hellenic flag. Our friend the sacristan came in, bearing mountains of leaf spinach which he had picked that very evening, and washed and cooked for us; he was a former refugee from Asia Minor, teasingly called "Father Inönü" by his fellows and had never left the Holy Mountain in over forty years. Dish after dish followed: rice pilaff with mushrooms, various forms of macaroni, all piping hot and, wonder of wonders, a delicious omelette skirted with *pommes frites*. Every few minutes yet another benign figure appeared, carrying plates of salads, sliced cucumber, boiled lentils, carrots and *aubergines*, nuts of different kinds, olives, grapes and enormous black cherries, and then took his place along the wall to join in the general banter and encourage the guests. Here, indeed, was one of those "happy convents, bosom'd deep in vines, where slumber abbots purple as their wines". However, it is only fair to note that the good monks had already partaken of their frugal commons before entertaining us and that, alas, the wine, so often the one redeeming feature of an Athonite supper, had soured.

Everything was done to ensure our comfort that evening and cauldrons of hot water were brought in relays. We washed and scrubbed and laundered. Suddenly the heavens broke and we just had time to rescue the clothes-line and pegs lent by our kind hosts before a storm of tropical intensity engulfed the monastery. Such a deluge as this must have wrecked the Persian fleet under its luckless commander, Mardonius, more than twenty-four centuries past. For the climate of this region partakes of a Balkan character quite unlike that of the arid Cyclades or Attica to the south. That night was the first and only time we were troubled by mosquitoes – of other and even more infamous little beasts we never had

50
Three aesthetic saints: left to right, St Paul the Theban, St Makarios the Roman, St Joannikios the Great at Vatopedi

anything to complain. Below the walls the jackals sounded their own acute problems.

The storm was still raging next morning, so we delayed our departure from this most friendly house until after luncheon, a more simple affair of beans but served hot and consumed in the old refectory with its long tables and wooden benches. Sitting apart from us in solitary state, wearing his headgear as Orthodox monks must do at all times in public and as Grenadier officers affect when they do not wish to be spoken to by others while they eat, was a pale and gigantic youth with long hair and rudimentary beard, resembling not so much his emancipated contemporaries in the English social scene of "mods" and "rockers" as those Spanish Hapsburgs of pallid features in the paintings of Velázquez. This was the youngest novice, a recruit of sixteen; the oldest monk here had died only the previous week, we were told, aged ninety-six.

We retraced the path below Philotheou, passed by the site of our picnic and along the shore by the forbidding walls of Iveron. Farther on the track grew stonier and harder to follow as we entered brushland. We stopped by the appropriately picturesque and dilapidated arsenal of Koutloumousiou – for inland monasteries all preserve their access to the sea – and Stavronikita.

The idiorrhythmic monastery of the Conquering Cross is without doubt the youngest, the smallest and the poorest. An earlier foundation by Nicephorus Stavroniketos, general of the warlike Emperor John Tzimisces, is said to have existed on this site, which commands the best view on this side of the peninsula, but the credit for its endowment is due to the Oecumenical Patriarch Jeremias I in 1540. Stavronikita, therefore, is the only Ruling Monastery on Athos to have been established *since* the fall of Constantinople and in the four centuries of its existence, so brief by local standards, its funds and its inhabitants have decreased to almost vanishing point. Discounting the tragic condition of the Russian cenobion of St Pantaleimon and of other smaller Slav houses not on the establishment as Ruling Monasteries, this will probably be the first to crumble altogether into ruins and die. The gradual but relentless sequestration of monastic properties throughout the Balkans by nationalist governments during the last hundred years, the cataclysmic end of "Holy Russia" and overnight transformation of the largest, richest and most powerful supporter of militant Orthodoxy into the deadliest enemy of all religions, the laudable betterment in living conditions of the poorer peasants throughout the Christian East, accompanied by the erosion of faith by a materialist world, these are the factors that contribute to the eclipse. Droves of tourists, while they embarrass the resources of the remaining monks and disturb the quiet of centuries, may in the end provide the means to preserve the skeletons of at least the most famous, most historical and perhaps the most beautiful of these ancient institutions, but by then the danger is that all the original life will have gone, and the peninsula will contain a series of hotels catering for the young of all ages and sexes, perhaps one large museum housed centrally in the Protaton and all the wealth of timber and wild life given over to insecticide and fertiliser.

In 1964 the population of Stavronikita was reduced to eight monks, each with his own kitchen and separate apartments, for this is an idiorrhythmic abode. A service was in progress in the diminutive katholikon, dedicated to that most commonly popular of saints, "Santa Claus", Nicholas the Wonder-worker of Nicaea, so we crept in to peep at his icon, distinguished by an oyster shell stuck on the forehead, as it was found when drawn out of the sea in a fishing-net. We left a small contribution, drank from the pump and went on.

Pantocratoros, the idiorrhythmic monastery consecrated to the Almighty, occupies the top of a rocky promontory overlooking a Lilliputian harbour. From the entrance gate there is a wonderful view of Stavronikita on its own headland between two little bays against the long, tent-shaped silhouette of the peak. Founded in 1357 by two noblemen and officials of the Byzantine court, Alexius *the Stratopedarch* and John *the Primicerius*, it was restored in 1536 by Barboulos *the Logothetes* of Ugro-Wallachia. The sloping courtyard is enclosed by buildings and in the upper part is the church of the Transfiguration, which is of the deepest, purplish red, almost loganberry, and contains frescoes of 1538 that include work of such remarkable quality that they are attributed to Panselinos.

We had become trained by now to look for the scenes from the Bible and portraits of prophets, saints and benefactors in the exact and appropriate places as ordained in the *Painters' Guide*, written in 1458 by Dionysius, a monk of Zographou. Always in the centre of the main dome the stern features of Christ in the Byzantine concept of Judge on high looked down upon us, and the Dormition of the Virgin could be discerned opposite the iconostasis on the wall over the doorway from the narthex. We began to recognise the special canon of Athonite saints, patrons and prototypes of asceticism. First of all the Egyptians, starting with St Anthony, the pioneer of Christian hermits and St Pachomius, the founder of monachism, St Makarios of the *danse macabre*; St Paul of Thebes, St Nilus and St Ephraim, St Moses and St Onophrius – he with the longest beard and most attenuated frame of all, the anchorite who lived alone in the desert for seventy years and from whose name the modern form, Humphrey, is derived. Next came the Syrians, the most extravagant exponents of self-denial, the "Pillar Saints", Simeon the Stylite and Daniel his follower, sometimes depicted in *trompe-l'œil*, standing or crouching above the capitals of the actual columns that support the fabric of the building. St Simeon, we read "bound a rope round him so that it became embedded in his flesh which putrified around it. A horrible stench, intolerable to the bystanders, exhaled from his body, and worms dropped from him whenever he moved. He built a pillar sixty feet high and scarcely a yard in circumference on which, during thirty years, he remained exposed to every change of climate. For a year St Simeon stood upon one leg, the other being covered with hideous ulcers, while his biographer was commissioned to stand by his side, to pick up the worms that fell from his body, and to replace them in the sores, the saint saying to the worm, 'Eat what God has given you.' From every quarter pilgrims of every degree thronged to do him homage. When he died a crowd of prelates followed him to the grave, and the general voice of mankind pronounced him the highest model of a Christian saint." [2] The series ends with the originators and particular heroes of monastic life on Athos: St Peter the Athonite, the precursor of all the anchorites on the Holy Mountain, who lived for thirty years in a cave here and crawled about on all fours grubbing roots, often portrayed next to St Onophrius (the latter's beard being even longer and almost touching the ground, presumably to indicate that he won on points for sheer endurance); the more historical figure of St Athanasius the Athonite, friend of emperors and founder of the Grand Lavra,

[2] Quoted from D. C. SOMERVELL's, *A Short History of Our Religion*, 1925, condensed from LECKY, *European Morals*, ii, p. 112. Amateurs of the macabre in religion may refer to my father's account of St Simeon on pp. 143–46 of *Arabesque and Honeycomb* (Sacheverell Sitwell, published by Robert Hale, 1957).

51
The scattered idiorrhythmic settlement of Kapsokalyvia

his supposed contemporary, St Paul of Xeropotamou with two foundations to his credit, and a host of other protectors, tutelary saints and exemplary inmates of the monasteries.

The red-bearded guest-master at Pantocratoros resembled an energetic young petty officer, for ever scrubbing the decks and making everything ship-shape. He gave us a good supper, if cold and vegetarian, and plenty of *raki*, but there was no wine. Situated anywhere else in the world, his monastery might well be thought outstanding, but among its neighbours there are many to rival Pantocratoros in beauty and interest.

We decided to return to Karyes and explore the other coast. Our cavalcade set off early to cross the high ground leading to the capital but this was our last journey with mules, for Angelos had suddenly demanded and as promptly been refused an exorbitant increase in fees. After a gruelling march in great heat, pondering on the workings of the peasant mind, we attained the crest of the ridge and spied Karyes lying in a coomb on the hillside. An hour later we were dumped unceremoniously at the café, where we had our usual "brunch" of eggs and honey. We saw Angelos on at least two further occasions at the *Ritz Bar* and were greeted by him cordially as old friends; he was still unemployed and lounging around happily enjoying his earnings without thought for the morrow. We took the motor-coach (registration number A01) through hazel woods over the spine of the peninsula, past the gloomy monastery of Xeropotamou to Daphni, the little port of blameless reputation and unsuitable name. We bathed a discreet distance away from monks and sea-urchins, bought a few tins and other provisions from the shops along the promenade and settled down at a table beneath the trellised wistaria outside the inn. During the war, according to the late Mr Sydney Loch in his most informative book *The Holy Mountain*, the top storey of this building was reserved for escaping Allied officers while German soldiers slept below. We made friends with the ecclesiastical gendarme, an elderly and pompous member of the corps, given to a little harmless braggadocio and armed with a heavy baton for beating down any inquisitive female heads that might dare to peep out from portholes of visiting yachts. Public transport arrived; it was the boat that plies around the peninsula twice a week and was to become the mainstay of our expedition now that we had parted from the muleteer. We

52
Hermit at Kapsokalyvia

G

joined a mixed party of monks and laity bound for the terminal point of Tripiti
and the world, and were soon chugging into the port of St Pantaleimon, the
vast Russian monastery with fantastic onion domes and derelict barracks. A
few minutes later we reached Xenophontos, which sprawls downhill to the   ILLS 38 & 43
shingle beach, so that here arsenal and gatehouse are combined in one.

The strict abbey of Xenophontos has endured the vicissitudes of at least nine
centuries. Ten years ago an English postulant was admitted, the son of an official
in the Ministry of Agriculture, but he did not stay. In 1964 we were to find
twenty-five monks all over seventy, so the prospects for this ancient and friendly
house are bleak. An earlier monastery consecrated to St George may have once
existed here but recorded history begins with a rebuilding by Stephen the
Eunuch, *Drungarius* or Admiral-in-Chief of the Byzantine Navy, with help from
his emperor, Nicephorus III Botaniates. Later the eunuch ended his days as
a monk here in a cell by the keep he built which survives. Two centuries there-
after the monastery was destroyed by pirates and was further restored in both
the sixteenth and eighteenth centuries by pious Moldo-Wallachian princes.
The most recent alterations took place after a fire in 1807, when the *New Katholikon* was added, so that Xenophontos possesses two main churches, both dedicated to St George, as well as nine chapels within its walls.

The *Old Katholikon* is supported by columns with ancient Corinthian capitals   ILL. 42
and is decorated with frescoes dated 1546 and attributed to the Cretan master
Theophanes. In a corner is the Chapel of St Demetrius, believed to be older than
the monastery itself. The frescoes continue with engaging representations of
fabulous animals in the passage leading to the refectory, where there are further
murals of earlier date but badly restored. Steps outside lead to a splendid
old mulberry tree and a large water cistern fed by a stream that runs under the
pavement and through the entire complex of buildings.

In what might be termed the "upper bailey" is the *New Katholikon*, containing
a remarkable collection of icons that show up well against the plain white interior. Most important are two mosaic portraits on facing panels attached to
columns, probably the most famous and beautiful works of art to remain on the
Holy Mountain today and which rightly made Robert Byron wax lyrical. The
figures are full-length and portray St George and St Demetrius, robed and

booted, against a background of gold. St George is attired in brown and St Demetrius in blue, and the garments of both are ornamented with intricate little patterns. The faces and hands are of particularly exquisite workmanship, as are the diminutive vignettes of Christ that appear as visions to each saint. These masterpieces are most likely of fourteenth-century date and are products of Constantinople. One writer points out that the artist aimed at making his work more effective from a distance; near inspection reveals the minute skills involved, but the vivid juxtaposition of colours so miraculously preserved in this medium through centuries can induce the same ugly rush of blood to the head that may be experienced by incautious close examination of modern art.

Costa's lumbago forced him to seek medical attention and he was led away for an injection by an immense cenobite with tangled beard and basso-profundo voice worthy to fill the part of Sarastro. Minutes later they emerged from what had proved a spotless and up-to-date surgery, happily discussing Patriarch, Pope and Peyrefitte. "Chaliapin" had practised as a doctor in Paris for ten years; he was a most charming and erudite member of a community that will live on our memory as one of the kindest and most welcoming of all. We spent one of our happiest evenings, chatting to the monks sitting on the benches in the covered gallery with its overhanging beams, ropes and windlasses. For supper we had the inevitable beans yet somehow even they tasted delicious, having been cooked in excellent olive oil. "We have a trained agronomist among us here," explained the saintly octogenarian guest-master. "But nobody wants to buy our oil, our wine, or fruit and vegetables any more," he added, sadly. Afterwards we sat on for a while on the little red-painted balcony outside our sitting-room, looking out over the neat plots of vegetables and the pebble shore, across the calm waters of the Singitic Gulf to the distant outline of Longos.

The Monastery of the Storekeeper, round the next bend in the coast, presents the largest, tallest and in some ways the finest church, and the most marvellous views. From the arsenal a short path lined with oleanders leads uphill past the gazebo to the porter's lodge, manned by a civilian, and into the courtyard, narrow and terraced to accommodate the huge katholikon for here, even more so than at neighbouring Xenophontos, architecture assails topography and the buildings are disposed against the steep contours of the escarpment.

The name of Docheiariou is derived from a traditional foundation by the Storekeeper of the Grand Lavra, St Euthymius, friend and contemporary of St Athanasius. The magnificent katholikon was erected in 1568 by order of Alexander IV Lapuşneanu, Voivode of Moldavia, and Roxandra, his wife, and the work was supervised by Theophanes, retired Bishop of Moldavia, who is buried here. The structure betrays certain specifically Moldavian features such as the buttresses and elongated drums upon which the domes are set. The slender proportions dictated as much by the restricted site as by canons of style, intensify the elegance and grace of the exterior and, as in French Gothic or perpendicular churches in western Europe, produce effects that are at once harmonious and awe-inspiring to the interior – enhanced as it is by extensive frescoes of felicitous execution. These paintings cover every inch of wall, arch and dome in the church proper, the unusually large narthex, the passage leading to the refectory and the refectory itself. The master originally responsible was another Cretan, named Zorzi, and if his work is largely restored this has been accomplished with skill and sympathy.

Docheiariou has had its fair share of supernatural phenomena, connected with the oratory of the Gorgoypecoos, situated off the refectory passage, where an icon bearing this difficult name is enshrined, and the phiale in the courtyard. The icon has enjoyed worship of peculiar zeal ever since the occasion in the seventeenth century when the Virgin reproved a negligent monastic butler for allowing the smoke of his candle to scorch her image, blinded him when he persisted, then later forgave him and restored his sight. The phiale, like the church, is dedicated to the Holy Archangels and is painted with stories of their intervention on behalf of those in trouble at sea, including a legend of especial significance. A shepherd boy on one of the monastery's farms on Longos discovered a buried treasure and informed the abbot, who sent over three monks to escort the boy and his find to Docheiariou. On the way the monks decided to murder poor Basil, for that was his name, and conceal the treasure to their own advantage, so they tied a lump of marble around his neck and threw him overboard. However, Basil cried in his distress to the archangels, who spirited him out of the sea and deposited him in the church, alive but soaking wet and with the stone still around his neck. Needless to add, the treasure was recovered, Basil forgave his

53
The Roumanian skete of the Prodromos

enemies and ended as abbot of Docheiariou, and the piece of marble is preserved to this day as one of the monastery's most cherished possessions. Such
stories may indeed be tedious, but they reflect the prevailing atmosphere and
figure prominently in the faith, physical surroundings, and life of the monks.

The terraced courtyard culminates in a splendid keep, perhaps equalled by
those at Chilandar and Karakallou, but dominating here as nowhere else. We
stood on the topmost level of ground beneath its walls to admire and photograph
the church in the foreground, the rising tiers of idiorrhythmic private apartments
on either side, many with neat little balconies and window-boxes to supplement
the green of the laurel shrubs around us and, over the tops of the roofs and past
the chimney-stacks, the blue of sea and sky.

In the evening we bathed by a disused anchorite's cave and then walked up the
hill and through the outbuildings to a beautifully kept vegetable garden, tended
by a rustic in a straw hat and a tall and distinguished-looking conventual over-
seer. We got into conversation: the monk was a nephew or cousin of the novelist
Nikos Kazantzákis, and was soon providing us with one of those haphazard
snacks so often better than any organised meal in Greece, an odd combination
of cucumber and mulberry culled on the spot. He pointed out the nest of a large
animal of nocturnal habits that haunts the enormous cypresses at the top of the
garden and we made our way back to the monastery, where Costa had arranged
for a mass to be sung for his mother.

Docheiariou is the last monastery on this coast before the frontier at Frango-
kastro ten miles away, but inland are various settlements we did not visit, including the two cenobitic monasteries of Kastamonitou and Zographou.

Kastamonitou lies in a wooded glen about two hours' march from Docheiariou. First mentioned in the eleventh century, it counts several emperors of
the Palaeologue dynasty and a Serbian princess, Anne the Philanthropic, among
benefactors. In 1433 the Serbian general Raditch restored the monastery before
retiring here as the monk Romanus. Since his time many of the abbots have
borne Slav names, and the dreary sequence of fires and chronic poverty has laid
it open to Russian financial help and political interference as at Esphigmenou and
other poorer foundations. One wing was constructed at the expense of Vassiliki,
Christian concubine of the notorious Ali Pasha of Yannina. For many years

54
Hermitages at Karoulia,
"Place of the Pulleys"

Kastamonitou was virtually abandoned until two monks from Sinai managed to raise sufficient funds from prolonged tours of Russia to complete the present buildings in the middle of the last century.

Zographou, Monastery of the Painter, lies among cypress plantations near the centre of the peninsula, and has remained a Bulgarian preserve throughout its long history since a reputed foundation by Moses, Aaron and John, three nobles of Ochrida, over a thousand years ago. Nothing remains of a great re-building programme by Moldavian princes of about 1500; the large courtyard contains two churches dated 1764 and 1801, and all else is later, including a monument to twenty-six monks said to have been burnt here by the *latinizers* of Michael VIII in 1274.

It was time for us to visit the Russians and, if the happiness of our brief sojourn at Docheiariou, Xenophontos and other monasteries was tempered by the thought of impending doom that surely confronts these venerable places of such historic interest and beauty, sheer tragedy met us at the Russian establishments. The vast and hideous St Pantaleimon that housed one thousand, five hundred monks around 1900, where Robert Byron found "pathos, almost tragedy in this deflation" to six hundred about thirty years later and which R. M. Dawkins described as "lamentable" in 1933, was reduced to thirty-four inmates, half of them bed-ridden, in June 1964; and its once prosperous dependency of Chromitsa, in farmland over against the frontier, which formerly boasted seven hundred inhabitants now contained one solitary caretaker monk. St Andrew's *skete*, a sub-sidiary of Vatopedi that held a thousand Russians in 1914, we found reduced to six.

The incredible conglomeration of neo–Byzantine erections commonly known as the Russiko and dedicated to Pantaleimon, martyr and tutelary saint of phy-sicians,[3] is the only foundation that the Russians, despite their pressures and intrigues, ever succeeded in controlling absolutely and raising to the status of a Sovereign Monastery. Earlier buildings on the site patronized by the Phanariote family of Callimachi had fallen into ruin, and were taken over and transformed with the help of the Tsars during the course of the nineteenth century. The

[3] The name of St Pantaleimon has come to spell vital security for more than half the world's population, outside Scotland. For "pants", whatever the local application of the term on opposing sides of the Atlantic, are derived from the *pantaloons* of a character in the "Commedia dell'Arte" named after this saint long popular in Venice as San Pantaleone.

55
Painter monk at the skete of St Anne's

results display that chaos and immensity of scale of most things connected with Russia, and can hardly be measured in terms of size, ugliness and misery.

We had left Docheiariou early and, after docking briefly at Xenophontos, went on here. A lay gendarme and a couple of ancient boatmen with pale skins and high cheek-bones met us at the quay, followed by one or two aged monks of similar features, while in the background hovered that diminutive scarecrow figure we had noticed on our outward journey two days previously, flitting along the water's edge, head bent beneath the weight of years and an enormous eye-shade, veering rapidly and noiselessly from boulder to boulder, stooping to examine washed-up timbers from the decaying roofs above, searching for the shifting colonies of sea-urchins, peering myopically at the new arrivals and then, on our approach, gliding off at speed, skirts billowing, to a distant cluster of rocks, like some demented Christian Sisyphus, condemned till the end of time to haunt these stony shores.

We clambered up to an ornate holy well and had a picnic breakfast, beneath the plane trees. Strengthened by coffee and morbid curiosity, we braced ourselves and continued the ascent. On reaching the gatehouse a Cossack-booted lay brother indicated the expected further climb up mouldering staircases, past huge and ramshackle edifices in various stages of disrepair into the mammoth guest-wing, constructed to accommodate hordes of Slavic pilgrims and now graced by a few idle and gawping tourists. We were shown into the assembly hall on the top storey with Bessarabian rugs on floor and tables and complete gallery of ILL. 60 Romanov portraits, and then chewed squares of Turkish delight on a rickety balcony overlooking the nightmare proliferation of cracked roofs and cupolas ILL. 35 of spiky onions topped with lemon globes and rusting crosses. We purchased rosaries and postcards, and made our descent to the katholikon, an exotic and most oppressive affair. Outside we found a monk of pronounced Mongolian countenance, very tall and fat, with thick black hair and scanty beard. In squeaky tones he proclaimed himself one of the four inmates of Greek blood, and that he was born at Taganrog in southern Russia. What diluted strain of Pontic Chersonite miscegenation with Petcheneg or Krim Tartar produced this stange individual it was useless to guess. Under his guidance we laboured upstairs once more to see an interior chapel of equal size and hideousness

56
A young novice at Karyes

to the first. Finally, we inspected the refectory, a cavernous chamber decorated with peeling repetitions of the admonitory scenes by now familiar. Some forty trestle tables and benches were displayed and at the end of one were places laid for ten. The thought of presuming on the hospitality of this pathetic remnant was too much, and we left with relief for the simple pleasures of Daphni.

We returned by the bus to Karyes for the last time. Nothing seemed to have changed, and all our old friends were in the café. Angelos and the "cherry-picker" monk with all the tin-openers volunteered to guard our belongings and we sauntered off to St Andrew's. This is one of the four cenobitic *sketes* planned and run like fully-fledged monasteries of the stricter variety, but lacking independent status or property beyond their walls, and ruled by a prior of the inmates' choosing under the feudal sway of a house on the "Establishment", in this case Vatopedi. Members of the next-door seminary view the surviving occupants of what is still unkindly nicknamed the "Seraglio" with slight pity and amused contempt. Visitors from the outside world, uninhibited by the age-old envy of the once opulent Slavs by their less numerous co-religionists to the south, cannot explore this skeleton of former glory and wander around its court-yards and into its many chapels without experiencing feelings of horror and depression, aggravated on encountering the residue of tenants, decrepit and gaga. One old dodderer showed us the katholikon, a well-proportioned building, famous for its painting of the Madonna and Child by that most busy of artists, St Luke, and housing an immense and elaborate cenotaph in which is encased a finger of St Andrew the Apostle. He explained that the key to the reliquary had been mislaid for many years and added that, since the last priest in the community here had died nineteen years ago, there had never been held a service in any one of the sixteen crumbling chapels. The seminarists told us later how the monk that cooked for his dwindling band of fellows had grown strange of late and for the past three years had no longer permitted anyone else to call on the ailing prior whose exact condition had therefore become a matter of speculation. They pointed to the fire-scorched timbers and gaping walls of one section that had been caused as a result, so they inferred, of a temporary decision to transfer cooking arrangements to the library which until then had contained numerous Russian and Glagolitic manuscripts. We were unable to find the room in which

ILL. 27

are stored the implements of self-mortification for which St Andrew's is renowned and, after high tea in the capital, retired to the "mod. cons." of Koutloumousiou for the night.

ILL. 49

On our way back to Daphni next morning we stopped at the Monastery of the Dry Torrent. Four-square and bleak, its origins obscured as much by the forgeries of its own historians as by the passage of time, idiorrhythmic Xeropotamou honours among benefactors, besides Palaeologue emperor and Wallachian hospodar, one of the greatest of Ottoman sultans, Selim I, conqueror of Syria and Egypt (born 1467, reigned 1512–20). The Forty Martyrs of Sebaste appeared in a vision to the Sultan and commanded him to rebuild this monastery and its church dedicated to their glory. The Grand Turk complied and six lamps hang in his memory before the icon of the Martyrs.[4] The present building, however, dates from the second half of the eighteenth century and was frescoed at the expense of funds raised by the monk and poetaster Kaisarios Daponte, who is also responsible for the phiale of marble from Chios and the verses around the rim of its basin, rendered by Mr R. M. Dawkins as follows:

> "I am Chian, if you ask me, I am a Chian dame;
>
> And so I am, as you may see, exceeding fair of fame;
>
> A daughter of Daponte; Kaisarios was his name;
>
> To where the river's fresh, not dry, he called me and I came;
>
> That men may see my beauty and loudly praise the same;
>
> And if you ask me what I am called: The Fountain is my name."

The greatest possession of Xeropotamou is its portion of the True Cross, thirteen inches long and the largest fragment on Athos. After the usual farcical delays in determining which monk was reponsible and running him to earth, we were shown this famous relic, shaped like the badge of Lorraine and encased in silvergilt. I confess I was irritated by some of the foregoing pantomime and must have betrayed Protestant foibles in according the exact degree of reverence enjoined

---

[4] Some confusion appears among writers on Athos as to whether indeed it was the terrible Selim I, murderer of his own father and brothers, or his grandson, another Selim, (born 1524, reigned 1566–74), described in Chambers' *Biographical Dictionary* as "a degraded sot" to whom the vision was vouchsafed. Selim II is known to have abandoned his pleasures on one occasion to make a state visit to the Holy Mountain, so he may well have had this experience on returning to normal routine.

by the sacristan, to his pious fury, and nervously enthused over the next treasure, the beautiful little Cup of Pulcheria, carved in green ophite with minute reliefs of the Virgin and Child, with angels and apostles, probably to be assigned to the eleventh century.

Incorporated into the wall of the exonarthex is a relief of St Demetrius of the fifth or sixth century, and a series of curious heads in classical style are set in like manner around the courtyard which contains a fine clock-tower some two hundred years old. We walked downhill from the main gate, photographing a Roumanian hermit and his mules en route and reached Daphni, where we lunched and caught the 2 p.m. boat for the Lavra.

ILL. 19

The sun beat down fiercely as we doubled a headland and came in sight of the gaunt silhouette of Simopetra perched on its crag half-way between heaven and abyss, and we drew into its arsenal with ancient watch-tower and spacious modern portico bewraying its proud reputation for poverty. Next followed in procession those monasteries we should visit on the last day of our expedition, the boat stopping at every little port and, as we progressed southwards, the mountain seemed to rise ever more steeply from the water's edge, the peak sometimes protruding from its plume of cloud nearly seven thousand feet above us. We came to the region of the sketes and hermitages, where the true ascetics follow the precepts and austerities of the earliest founders of Athos. Round another bend and the boatman pointed out the rocks where the Persian fleet had foundered. We swept past Karoulia, the Place of the Pulleys, a crow's nest of huts clinging to the cliff-side two hundred feet and more from sea-level, its only access a ladder of iron rings clamped into the rock from above, still inhabited by two or three Russians with a cave connected by rope into which they retreat from time to time for deeper meditation. We swung out again, passing an isolated rock topped with a chapel and came in below the large settlement of Kapsokalyvia, or the Burnt Huts, so-named from the habit of its founder St Maximos, who was also given to levitation at times, of destroying his shelters and moving on whenever he felt himself too comfortable. High on the mountainside clung a little group of cottages, each with domed chapel at its eastern end, like a scattered village round the central church, in this case termed a *kyriakon*, in the centre of the ravine. Suddenly from behind the rocks appeared a

ILL. 54

ILLS 51 & 52

57
Intimations of mortality on
a mountain path

crowd of hermits, many in sack-cloth and bare-footed but all sporting the regulation stove-pipe headgear and, led by a gnome scarcely four feet high, they began to tug and heave at the boat. Their provisions landed and a frenzied spot-check made, they vanished as quickly. The scenery seemed wilder at every turn. We reached Karavostasi, the Bay of the Standing Ship, where the Virgin indicated to St Peter the Athonite that he should land and scramble up the rocky scree to find his cave. Another heave and we saw the tiny white dot of the church inside the mouth of the cavern of St Athanasius. Every cliff and rock-face had its quorum of anchorites. We rounded Cape Akrathos and immediately the landscape seemed to lose its drama: we were on the eastern coast once more but far from the sheltered coves and forested shores of earlier explorations; here, as we neared the Lavra, there seemed no variation from rock and scrub.

The harbour of the Lavra with its mole dominated by the arsenal now garrisoned by civilian gendarmerie, its piles of timber waiting for transhipment and one or two fishing smacks riding to anchor, resembles that of Pantokratoros and, it may be, thousands of other little ports throughout the Mediterranean or even, as has been suggested, the coves and havens of Cornwall, except in one respect: the almost total stoppage of human activity. Perhaps it is the siesta hour before nones or a day in the calendar from which gainful occupations are precluded and yet this is the port of the Grand Lavra, the largest and wealthiest of all the Sovereign Monasteries of the Holy Mountain. The truth is that trade, along with the resources in skill, financial means and the physical strength and numbers of the monks, is ebbing out. We had better eat our tinned *dolmades*, drink our *retsina* and try to conjure up the barque of Ulysses approaching and agree on a suitable painter and apt quotation for the scene.

The Grand Lavra is the oldest, largest, richest, best-known and most holy monastery on Athos, and in some respects the most disappointing. Like most, it occupies a commanding position on the crest of a hill, its walls present the same sombre exterior with projecting wooden galleries but, once the steep road – I use this word advisedly to denote its superior surface – is ascended and the cork-screw passage into the interior is negotiated, anti-climax meets the traveller. A haphazard collection of buildings blocks the view and the seasoned Athonite wanderer misses the immediate impact of blood-red church and stately cypress

58
The percussion tower at Dionysiou with bells and fixed semandra. The clock above with one hand and Turkish numerals, shows Athonite time

that the humblest of other houses have to offer; the majestic proscenium of
Vatopedi might be on another planet. Herein lies, of course, the subtle difference
between each monastery, all built to a rigid plan, yet varied according to the
circumstances dictated by topography and history. The Lavra derives strength
from its aura of antiquity and prestige; one feels that if all the daughter houses
are emptied and fall into ruin, and their lands snatched by greedy secular powers,
somehow this place, the fountain and archetype will never dry up and wither
away; there will always be a few young men, misfits in the modern world,
sufferers of personal tragedy or spiritual upheaval, ambitious for preferment in
their church, or genuine followers of the vocation who will come here to tread
in the steps of Athanasius. And, of course, the church and tomb, and the relics
associated with the Saint and with the rival emperors who supported him must
always be worth a visit.

The katholikon of the Grand Lavra is the type and model of all the churches
on Athos, excepting the Protaton, and its lines if not fabric are as laid down by St
Athanasius. Nevertheless, expectations are not fulfilled: the interest remains
historical or iconographical, rather than aesthetic. The squat dome and garish
verandah that has replaced the ancient narthex give warning. The interior is im-
pressive in atmosphere rather than in style or detail: the walls have been frescoed
throughout and according to book, and have never been restored since completion in 1535 by the Cretan Theophanes but, whereas in the simple surroundings of Xenophontos his work has charm if not great power, here it is altogether
too restrained, hieratic and almost banal; neither does the heavy marble iconostasis help. There is nothing to compare with, say, Assisi. Nor is this comparison
altogether unfair, if one considers the relative importance of the two saints to
their respective branches of the Christian faith, or reflects on the wonders of
Byzantine art that have survived the random fate of history. Here one must be
content with a few particulars, the portraits of the founder's patrons, who con-
front each other in the full glory of their imperial trappings from opposing
pillars in the nave, the murdered Nicephorus Phocas adorned with a halo and
bearing the original charter of foundation, his assassin and supplanter in bed and
throne, John Tzimisces, holding a model of the church. Let us rather dwell on
the spiritual associations of these hallowed precincts where lie the mangled re-

59
Gregoriou

mains of the great Athanasius who, after all his struggles against the wiles of the flesh and the devil, was crushed by the masonry of his own church.

The *trapeza*, or refectory, opposite the church and the *phiale* and two cypresses between these buildings are more rewarding. The trees were planted by St Athanasius and his bursar, St Euthymius, founder of Docheiariou; sad to relate one has now succumbed after a thousand years. The phiale, immense, secular and barbaric, displays a hotch-potch of styles, Turkish dome and pillars and Byzantine or oriental basin with curious carved motifs of animals, and is justly an object of pride to the monks and speculation to scholars. A battery of semandra to augment the carillon from the neighbouring bell-tower and columns from an ancient city on this site ornament the entrance to the refectory. Inside all is dark and gloomy; the small windows admit not much light to discern the grim series of murals, dating from the construction in 1512 by Gennadius, Archbishop of Serres. There is a fine Dormition of St Athanasius and a Tree of Jesse, but harrowing scenes of martyrdom and gaunt figures of ascetic saints prevail, and the Last Judgement contains a particularly horrendous representation of Hell as Leviathan belching torrents of flame. Small wonder that the monks have chosen to release themselves from the cenobitic rule and take their meals in privacy.

In order to see the treasury we left the dormitory we shared with seven others at five in the morning, to meet the monks responsible as they ended matins. First we walked past refectory and church to a small chapel at the far end of the courtyard where a great number of icons are hung as in a gallery, many of minute size and intricate workmanship but few earlier than the fourteenth century. The manuscripts with a number of *chrysobuls* and printed books are housed in separate sections of a modern building near by. The collection of bishop's "crowns", crosses and reliquaries next door again are more interesting, and include the famous Bible of Phocas, an admirable portable mosaic and a cup that belonged to the Nicene emperors. We passed by the tombs of patriarchs buried in the courtyard and visited the Chapel of St John Koukouzelis, a great singer. After breakfast in the sixteenth-century guest-wing we set off for the Cave of St Athanasius at ten o'clock.

We were back in the wilderness. Soon the olives and patchy vegetable fields

60
Gallery of Romanov portraits in the reception room at the Russian monastery of St Pantaleimon

61
The guest-master of St Paul's

were behind and we toiled on through woods of holly and arbutus. Every few miles we came to an ornamental fountain head and water trough, a wayside cross or the unsigned meeting of another stony track, but we kept on with the sea on our left and the towering mass of the peak on our right. We reached a more level stretch of paving and found ourselves at the gate of the Prodromos, the cenobitic skete of the Roumanians dedicated to the Baptist, and an appanage of the Lavra which in fact owns most of the well-named Desert of Athos around the precipitous end of the promontory. The Prodromos is, therefore, in the same category and sad condition as St Andrew's and the two other cenobitic sketes which we did not visit, the Bulgarian Bogoroditsa ("Mother of God"), near Vatopedi, but belonging to St Pantaleimon and the Russian Skete of the Prophet Elijah, in the hills behind Pantokratoros to which it belongs. However, if the inmates are all fast approaching their end and are in rags and extreme want, they lack nothing in kindliness and hospitable instincts. We were welcomed by a doddering old guest-master who insisted on according us all the usual civilities and chatted amiably without betraying a hint of the pathos and misery of his circumstances. We visited their church, touchingly painted by painstaking artists   ILL. 53
of the Victorian era and showing signs of imminent ruin, and asked permission to eat our picnic on the benches under the cypress. At first they pressed us to share their commons; then conceded that, after all, they had not been expecting company and readily consented to our plan, the host shambling off to fetch knives, mugs and platters. Another old gaffer clumped up to us with beakers of wine, while a third appeared from the vegetable garden they have made for themselves inside the courtyard and beamingly presented his best cucumbers. In turn we left most of our remaining supplies, but they refused any kind of payment, although that is normally expected anywhere on Athos outside of the twenty ruling houses. Never will I forget those kind old men.

We dozed in the niches along the entrance passage and then took our way again. The vegetation changed; hollies and stunted firs gave way to scrub and broom and we came to a little group of stone huts with conical roofs at one end, similar to what we had seen from the sea. These were *kalyves*, dwellings of anchorites, sometimes isolated communities of only a very few monks such as at Karoulia, the Place of Pulleys, depending directly on one of the twenty monasteries, or organised into one of the nine so-called idiorrhythmic *sketes*, like Kapso-kalyvia, which are ruled by a Prior responsible to a monastery. Less severe than the ascetic *kalyves* are the *kellia*, which resemble farmhouses and are ruled by an Elder who reports direct to a monastery, or the *kathismata*, which are rented for life from a ruling house and approximate to country villas.[5] We found a resident and he led us to the abode of the guardian of the cave. The latter turned out to be a sprightly young man of twenty-three, who had led this strange and austere life since the age of eighteen, and proceeded to lead us at great speed along a track through the gorse, sinister beings scudding or slithering back into the undergrowth at every pace. Indeed, apart from their presence the landscape of rock and sparse, prickly vegetation, the stone walls, bee-hive huts and wooden crosses marking the way with the ever-present mountain above, reminded one of western Ireland. Suddenly we were on top of a precipice hundreds of feet above the Bay of the Standing Ship. Two hundred steps led down the cliff-face to a ledge below the cave. On a fig tree in the tiny vegetable garden were votive offerings, rags fluttering in the breeze. The cave in fact contains two churches, the outer one dedicated to St Nicholas and the inner to the Virgin. Here is preserved the icon miraculously revealed to St Athanasius, which had traversed over the seas from Jerusalem, whence it had called a whore of Alexandria to repentance. Forswearing her sinful life she retired to the desert beyond Jordan for forty-seven years, where she died and was buried by a lion, becoming known to hagiologists as St Mary of Egypt. We returned, stopping to photograph the fantastic view of sea and mountain and stumbled on an eyrie right on the edge, with heavy stones anchoring the wooden slats of roof below us. A short track fit for chamois and a ladder led to a plot of beans in a recess quarried out of the precipice. Shouts above came from the robust figure of a veteran hermit; he had lived here for nearly forty years, the last twenty-five by himself, was an intelligent being and, like most of his race, intensely interested in politics. He accompanied us part of the way back. In three hours' time we reached the Lavra again with its hysterical guest-master and appalling lavatories, now to be shared by a hundred or so extremely smart young officers of the Greek Army.

[5] A detailed account of the various forms of monastic establishment appear in *The Monks of Athos*, by R. M. DAWKINS, to whom I am grateful for this information.

SACRED COUNCIL   KARYES, May 30th, 1964
OF THE HOLY MOUNTAIN

Ref. No 839

LICENCE OF STAY

to

The Twenty Sacred and Reverend Monasteries
of the Holy Mountain

The bearer of the present letter, bearing the Sacred Seal of our committee and duly signed, Mr Sacheverell Reresby Sitwell, Viscount, and English merchant, recommended to us by the Ministry of Foreign Affairs to photograph valuable objects in the monasteries, with a permit to stay twenty days, has arrived to visit the Sacred houses and worship before the holy and revered objects of our faith that are contained in them.

You are, consequently, requested to afford him in addition to a courteous welcome, every possible hospitality and attention towards the fulfilment of the purpose for which he has come here.

We remain with warm affection, your brothers in Christ.

The Supervisors of the Sacred Community of Holy Mount Athos.
Chief Supervisor Isaev Nuvakov of Chilandar Monastery
Supervisor Elder Constantinos of Xeropotamou Monastery
Supervisor Elder Demetrios of Saint Paul Monastery
Supervisor Elder Andreas of Gregoriou Monastery

ENVELOPE

THE ROMAN PATRIARCHATE
H. Fener – Istanbul
TURKEY

To the Holy Houses on the Holy Mountain

62
Licence to stay
granted by the
Supervisors of the
Sacred Community
of the Holy Mount
Athos; and an
envelope

ΚΑΡΥΑΙ ΤΗ 30ῇ Μαΐου 1964

ΔΙΑΜΟΝΗΤΗΡΙΟΝ

ΠΡΟΣ

ΤΑΣ ΕΙΚΟCΙΝ ΙΕΡΑC ΚΑΙ CΕΒΑCΜΙΑC ΜΟΝΑC
ΤΟΥ ΑΓΙΟΥ ΟΡΟΥC
ΑΘΩ

Ὁ κομιστὴς τοῦ παρόντος Ἱεροκοινοσφραγίστου καὶ ἐνυπογράφου γράμματος ἡμῶν

κ. Sacheverell Reresby Sitwell

Ὑποκόμης Ἄγγλος Ἔμπορος

συνιστώμενος ἡμῖν ὑπὸ τοῦ Ὑπουργείου τῶν ἐξωτερικῶν πραγμιτογράφων Κεφαλιακῶν ἀλλοτερίων μὲ ἄδειαν παραμονῆς 20 ἡμέρων

ἀφίκετο πρὸς ἐπίσκεψιν τῶν Ἱερῶν Σκηνωμάτων καὶ προσκύνησιν τῶν ἐν Αὐτοῖς ἀποκειμένων Ἱερῶν καὶ Ὁσίων τῆς Πίστεως ἡμῶν.

Παρακαλεῖσθε ὅθεν, ὅπως παράσχητε αὐτῷ, πρὸς τῇ φιλόφρονι ὑποδοχῇ καὶ πᾶσαν ἅμα δυνατὴν φιλοξενίαν καὶ περιποίησιν πρὸς ἐκπλήρωσιν τοῦ δι' ὃν ἔρχεται αὐτόσε σκοποῦ.

'Εφ' ᾧ καὶ διατελοῦμεν λίαν φιλάδελφως ἐν Χριστῷ ἀδελφοὶ

Οἱ Ἐπιστάται τῆς Ἱερᾶς Κοινότητος τοῦ Ἁγίου Ὄρους Ἄθω

Ὁ Χιλανδαρίου	Πρωτεπιστάτης	...
» Ξηροποτάμου	Ἐπιστάτης	...
» Ἁγίου Παύλου	»	...
» Ἐσφιγμένου	»	...

RUM PATRİKHANESİ
H. Fener — Istanbul
Türkiye

Τῇ Ἱερᾷ Κοινότητι Ἁγίου Ὄρους

Εἰς Ἅγιον Ὄρος

Next day we bathed near the arsenal and had our last picnic. I put away my portable cooker and we took the boat back round to the other coast again and landed at the Skete of St Anne.

The track up the mountainside was the roughest and most precipitous path and up the steepest gradients I have ever managed. In fact, one or two fellow-travellers who had tacked on to us at the Lavra found it too much for them and slithered back to the landing-stage to wait for the next boat. We of stouter heart persisted, clinging on for life to rocks and overhanging branches, thankful for the precocious fertility of the region. Everywhere the splash of water added to our difficulties but enriched the sights and sounds of our new whereabouts. We found the prosperous hide-out of two painter-hermits, one a deaf-mute. The incomparable view from their well-furnished house looked out over a garden of dahlias. They showed us their studio and we photographed one at work on his latest best-seller, an Annunciation of liquorice sentiment and colouring. After nips of raki and Turkish coffee and long draughts of water, we paid our respects to their chapel and left. Another back-breaking hour and we came to a humbler retreat of wood-carvers, then reached the main church and reception centre of the *skete*, which dates back to the sixteenth century and consists of about sixty or seventy cottages in all. More *raki* and we were taken round the church which is finely situated in a position dominating the ravine but resembles in every other way the normal pattern of Athonite churches. Its main treasure is what Robert Byron succinctly describes as "the left foot of the grandmother of God". Another long trek, passing the New Skete far below us and we reached the wide valley in which is the Monastery of St Paul.

St Paul's occupies a picturesque site on a ledge of rock overlooking a boulder-strewn ravine, against the barren back-cloth of the great mountain. Like all the monasteries on this, the harsher, western coast, with the exception of Xeropotamou with which it claims early associations and Docheiariou, it has retained the stricter way of life of a *cenobion*. The monks point to the exceptional qualities of leadership of their present abbot to account for their success in continuing to attract recruits, so that the current population of forty-two (in 1964) makes this the third in numbers although a comparatively unimportant monastery in history and other respects.

In early times St Paul's was inhabited by Serbian and Bulgarian monks, and the great Serbian warrior prince George Brankovitch built a church here in 1447. The circumstances of his daughter, the Sultana Mara's attempt to hand in person the relics of the Magi to this monastery are related in the first part of this book. Roumanian and Russian help succeeded in the following centuries but all the buildings, apart from the great tower built in 1522 and the crenellated wall, that protects the monastery from the mountainside above, are later even than the plain modern katholikon finished in 1844, with one notable exception. That is the little upstairs chapel of St George, with frescoes by a Constantinopolitan artist named Andronicus and belonging to the fifteenth or sixteenth century. Formerly ranking with the finest on Athos, they are now in a lamentable condition.

We enjoyed one of our best suppers here on our last evening on the Mountain, eaten in the same room as it was prepared and in company of a visiting wood merchant. The potency of the *raki* and the smell of carbolic in the wide ILL. 61 passages were as strong as Robert Byron and his companions noticed nearly forty years earlier. We were woken by the loud tattoo of the semandron beating round the church in the early hours and the sad thought of our self-enforced exile and brief continence coming to an end spoilt our relative comfort.

Once more we were up at dawn and trundled down the ravine to the arsenal to embark for Dionysiou, unique survival of the Trapezuntine empire. ILLS 47 & 48

Founded in 1375 by the Grand Comnenus Alexius III, Emperor of Trebizond, and still preserving the original *chrysobul*, Dionysiou takes its name from a hermit, Dionysius of Kastoria, who saw a mysterious light on this isolated rock and obtained the interest of his brother Theodosius, Metropolitan of Trebizond and through him the approbation and generosity of his august patron. Five centuries have passed since the extinction of that distant Pontic realm, the fissiparous offshoot of Byzantium, nurtured by the Comnenian dynasty on rich silver mines and trade with the East. Despite civil wars and the rival factions of the Amytzantarants and Scholarians, the Trapezuntine empire was destined to outlive the final siege of Constantinople itself for eight years, now the paintings and mosaics of its churches are slighted and the last generation of its Christian citizens are grown old in exile but here, on a remote pinnacle of the Holy Mountain, prayers are still intoned for repose of the good emperor's soul and that of his wife Theodora.

Along the upper storeys on the seaward side are the usual wooden balconies projecting out over the stonework and here, in these cramped surroundings an essential part of the general plan, providing access around the building and *every* other kind of convenience to inmates. Overlooking the arsenal is a modern block rising from concrete struts but, as the path winds round to the gate on the landward side, the handsome keep dated 1520 and solid masonry of this façade give this monastery more than any other the appearance of a medieval stronghold. The narrow confines of the rock base allow very little space around the brilliant red katholikon; one end of the cramped courtyard is taken up by an

ILL. 58

imposing percussion tower housing bells and semandra, and built in Italianate style but with Turkish numerals on its clock-face to further the difficulties of deciphering Athonite hours, and the whole of the south side between church and refectory is occupied by a painted cloister where the monks take macabre pleasure in pointing out to strangers the earliest portrayal of a mushroom cloud. This Trapezuntine foundation has been lucky in that since one disaster in 1535 it has been miraculously preserved from fires. The katholikon and its frescoes are dated 1547 and are due to that same Peter Rareş, Hospodar of Moldavia who endowed Karakallou and died as a monk there: the portrait of his wife is one of the few representations of normal child-bearing women to be found in these parts. The paintings in the refectory date from 1603 but might well be earlier, such is the force of tradition. The fact that they have survived fire and further restoration and that the refectory is in constant daily use adds to their interest. A recondite thrill may be had in speculating on the identity of a crowned figure among the line of ascetic saints and heroes. Is this not Joasaph, the Hermit King, second founder of the Great Meteoron in Thessaly, or is he that tiresome old Cantacuzene after all?

The greatest interest at Dionysiou, however, must remain centred on the magnificent *chrysobul*, now sensibly exposed to visitors through a protective glass but always in the presence of four or five watchful monks. In the words of George Finlay, the parchment is "a foot and a half broad and fifteen feet long, surrounded by a rich border of arabesques. The imperial titles are set forth in capitals about three inches high, emblazoned in gold and ultramarine; and the word Majesty, wherever it occurs in the document, is always written like the emperor's signature, with the imperial red ink."[6] Christ extends both hands to bless the figures of the Emperor and Empress, sixteen inches high, and below appear the imperial children in all the solemnity of childhood enriched by the knowledge of their inheritance.[7]

The Monastery of St Gregory of Sinai, a short distance by sea from Dionysiou, occupies a platform of rock rather less dramatic than its neighbour's and likewise claims a fourteenth-century foundation, although its origins are more obscure. Less fortunate than Dionysiou, it has suffered repeated fires and has several times been repaired by the Moldo-Wallachian princes. All the present buildings were constructed in the last decades of either the eighteenth or nineteenth century and are of very undistinguished aspect; a lot of white railings and overhanging ropes combine with the setting to give a distinctly nautical air. This is one of the clean-est and best-kept houses and the guest-wing where we were briefly entertained displays that unfailing good taste and feeling for décor that had impressed us everywhere.

ILL. 59

One monastery, apart from Zographou and Kastamonitou, remained un-visited and that perhaps the most famous of all, Simopetra. However, time was running short and both my companions had made the gruelling ascent on pre-vious occasions, so I contented myself with a solitary climb to a half-way shrine. In fact, since everything at Simopetra was destroyed by a ghastly and final con-flagration in 1893, there is little worth seeing apart from the view which is no

[6] G. FINLAY, *A History of Greece from its Conquest by the Romans to the Present Time* (146 B.C. to A.D. 1864), Vol. IV, Chapter 3, p. 384, London, 1877.

[7] A description of Manuel III, son of Alexius III, is contained in the following passage:

On the following day which was Saturday the Emperor called for us ambassadors, sending horses to bring us to his palace. On arrival we found him in a chamber that was off a gallery, where he received us very graciously and after talking with him for a space we returned to our lodging. At this audience after having speech with the Emperor we were presented to his son, who was a young man some twenty-five years of age. The Emperor is a man well-built, tall and of a stately presence; he and his son were dressed in imperial robes, wearing hats of a very high shape, which had cordings of gold running up the sides with a great plume on the top made of crane feathers; further these hats were trimmed with marten fur. The Emperor's name is Manuel and his son is called Alexius. They speak of the son too, like his father, as the Emperor, for this is their custom that the eldest son, who is heir to the Empire, yet during the lifetime of his father and like him, is called Emperor: and in the Greek tongue the title is Basileus. . . .

R. GONZALEZ DE CLAVIJO, *Embassy to Tamerlane, 1403–1406*. Translated from the Spanish by G. LESTRANGE, Cambridge, 1928, Chapter 6.

better than many from other points of the mountain. Better, said Costa and John Julius, admire the prodigious noble prospect from afar. However, I determined to get a little closer and plunged off into the undergrowth, camera at the ready. After all, the opportunity might never occur again, and what would the future hold for Simopetra and its less spectacular fellows? Gradual decay and extinction of monasteries and monks and perhaps some move from the outside world to encroach on the last of their lands and privileges. Simopetra, in particular, has always been a poor monastery, and its very position attracts numerous tourists who must inflict a considerable burden on dwindling strength and resources. The traditional free welcome and hospitality accorded to all-comers may be an entrenched clause in the charters, but it is often abused by those seeking a cheap holiday and was originally intended for the succour of pilgrims, not stray agnostics. One solution might be to discriminate between the genuine Orthodox pilgrims and others, who would be asked to pay not only for the privilege of obtaining their *Diamonitirion* but also be asked to make a fixed contribution at every monastery they wish to stay. The ancient convent of St Catherine at Mount Sinai now imposes a tax on all visitors of one Egyptian pound per night and, since its estates have been taken away this is the only source of income of the monks and their Bedu servants.

ILL. 63

I gained the summit of a great fold of rock and reached the shrine, where I stopped to rest mind and body. Ever in front and aloft loomed the elusive monastery. I must turn and go back, but first gaze a little at this unforgettable attempt of man to meet his God, the first sky-scraper with its tiers of balconies frowning over the abyss. Other and more fluent writers have described Simopetra athwart its mountain crag, like the deserted convents of Meteora and yet resembling in architecture the great barracks of the Potala, lost palace of the God-King of Tibet.

The Rock of St Simon-Flowing-with-Myrrh was first built over by a hermit of that name with aid from the Serbian prince John Ugljesa in 1363, and was originally known as the New Bethlehem, from the dedication of its church to the Nativity. Like the monasteries of the Meteora, which it resembles more than its neighbours, except perhaps for Dionysiou, it owes much to Serbian influence in early times and was for long predominated by monks of Slavonic race. Subsequent history has been terrible in the extreme owing to its position which has allowed no escape from the continual series of fires that have swept over it, in 1581, 1635 and 1893. And, despite frequent help from both Roumanians and Russians Simopetra has twice been closed through poverty in the eighteenth century and again, after the War of Greek Independence in 1821, when it suffered from occupation by the Turkish Army.

I clambered downhill again and joined the others on the boat for Daphni, and "the world". Suddenly the quiet pattern of our days was over and we were back in the noise and tensions of the twentieth century.

Bibliography

BYRON, R. *The Station*, London, 1928.

CHOUKAS, M. *The Black Angels of Athos*, London, 1935.

CURZON, R. *Visits to the Monasteries of the Levant*, London, 1849.

DAWKINS, R. M. *The Monks of Athos*, London, 1936.

HASLUCK, F. W. *Athos and its Monasteries*, London, 1925.

HUSSEY, J. M. "Byzantine Monasticism", *History*, June 1939.

LAKE, KIRSOPP, *The Early Days of Monasticism on Mount Athos*, Oxford, 1937.

LOCH, S. *The Holy Mountain*, London, 1957

LOVERDO, C. DE *J'ai été Moine au Mont Athos*, Paris, 1956.

MILLET, G. *Les Monuments de l'Athos*, Paris, 1927.

PERILLA, F. *Le Mont-Athos*, Paris, 1928.

RILEY, A. *Athos, or the Mountain of the Monks*, London, 1887.

SHERRARD, P. *Athos*, Oxford, 1960.

TALBOT RICE, D. "The Monasteries of Mount Athos", *Antiquity*, December 1928.

WARE, T. R. *The Orthodox Church*, London, 1963.

ZERNOV, N. *The Eastern Church*, London, 1961.

ACKNOWLEDGEMENTS

The authors and publishers would like to thank The Condé Nast Publications Ltd for their permission to reprint a passage from "The Holy Mountain" by Reresby Sitwell which appeared in the Winter 1964 number of *Wine & Food*.

The endpaper map was drawn by T. Stalker Miller

Index

Page numbers in **bold** indicate illustrations

Erissos

Frontier (no females beyond here)

CHILANDAR

ESPHIGMENO

ZOGRAPHOU

Ouranopolis

Chromitsa

Thebaid

Ammouliane

AMMOULIANE

Miles
0   1   2   3   4   5

Kilometres
0 1 2 3 4 5 6 7 8